What People Are Saying About
The Pink Steering Wheel Chronicles

"How do you get past grief? Laura Fahrenthold drove through it with her two daughters, facing down everything from a hungry alligator to a broken heart while scattering her beloved husband Mark Pittman's ashes across North America—and then some. The story would be sad if it weren't so hilarious. And hilarious if it weren't so sad. In the end, they reconnect in eerie, unexpected and surprisingly moving ways."

> —Amanda Bennett, Pulitzer Prize-winning author and investigative journalist

"In a memoir that is funny and heartfelt, Laura Fahrenthold lives with the grief of losing her husband—the love of her life and her daughters' father. Her humor and buoyancy invigorate their family's unconventional approach to mourning and carry the reader forward with a faith that even a relationship cut short by death can continue to sustain us."

> —Heather Harpham, author of *Happiness: The Crooked Little Road to Semi-Ever After*

"Laura Fahrenthold has constructed a jewel. We don't die anymore; we pass. *The Pink Steering Wheel Chronicles,* in its courage, gives us life everlasting."

> —Tom Keene, editor-at-large for Bloomberg News and host of Bloomberg Surveillance

"Incredible. A brutally honest, fast-moving and ultimately transcendent book about love's life after death."

—David Fahrenthold, *Washington Post* reporter, 2017 Pulitzer Prize winner

"A most personal and profound book teaching us that the facts of life are often found in dealing with death. Not just the part that's filled with pain and sorrow, but the other part, the one filled with rejoicing and honoring. And loving.

The Pink Steering Wheel Chronicles is remarkable not just for how Laura handled her husband's sudden death, but for the journey she takes us on afterwards...A road trip of the heart. And a bright light for the road that lies ahead for all of us."

—Bill Ritter, WABC-TV *Eyewitness News* anchor

"Most women, when they lose their husbands unexpectedly, are paralyzed by grief. Laura Fahrenthold—whose award-winning journalist husband succumbed to a heart attack before her eyes—got moving. With her two young daughters in tow, she decided to move forward—literally. She packed them all into an RV and proceeded to adventure across America and Canada, scattering her husband's ashes for four summers. The result? A journey of self-discovery and renewal, love and hope, punctuated by grieving in the arms of Walmart and Costco shoppers. Go ahead: take the ride!"

—Barbara Hoffman, Arts Editor, *The New York Post*

"Laura Fahrenthold tells the story of her husband's death with unflinching honesty and a sincere vulnerability that makes you want to reach through the pages to hug her. She uses those same skills to tell the story of his death's aftermath, loading her bereft daughters into a used RV and crossing North American to spread his ashes, all the while teaching her kids to stand on their own whether on top of a mountain or in a valley below. Along the journey, she teaches us about grief, motherhood, humor and strength, revealing that such great loss can bring with it surprising gifts."

—Ellen Wulfhorst, Chief Correspondent, Americas, Thomson Reuters Foundation

"Laura Fahrenthold tackles grief and loss in the most American of ways, hitting the road in a camper with two kids, a dog and her dead husband's ashes. Courageous, brutally honest and observant, *The Pink Steering Wheel Chronicles* is a classic road story of love and healing. It's also laugh-out-loud funny."

—Barbara Barker, *Newsday*

"*The Pink Steering Wheel Chronicles* is proof that loss isn't just about endings but also, if you're lucky, about beginnings.

Laura Fahrenthold perfectly describes what Buddhists call a *bardo*, a transition from one state of being to another. She reminds us that new beginnings don't come for free, but they do come. You just need the courage to get behind the wheel...and drive your way through it, one sprinkle of ashes at a time."

—Dean Starkman, author of *The Watchdog That Didn't Bark: The Financial Crisis and the Disappearance of Investigative Journalism*

"Imagine a road trip with courage guru Brene Brown and *Travels With Charley* author John Steinbeck. *The Pink Steering Wheel Chronicles* is that book: an endearing, sob and literally laugh out loud story of loss and hope that leaves you totally in awe of the human spirit. I could not put it down."

> —Robyn O'Brien, financial and food industry analyst and author of *The Unhealthy Truth*

"For anyone who needs a road map with which to navigate heartache, this book is it. Laura Fahrenthold shows with laudable humor and compelling honesty that sometimes all it takes is an open heart, an adventurous spirit, two willing daughters, and an RV with a pink steering wheel to get there."

> —Helaine Olen, author of *Pound Foolish* and co-author of *The Index Card*

"The list of things we're never taught about, but should be, is ridiculously long. Birth, marriage, taxes and death are a few of the biggies. Take a lesson right now from Laura Fahrenthold, on loss and grief, and how to move forward, not just with courage, but also with humour. Revel in it, remember it, pass it on, and when you one day have to find your way through it, you'll be just a little better equipped."

> —Sue Fitzmaurice, international coach and author of *Purpose*

"*The Pink Steering Wheel Chronicles* is beautifully written and profoundly moving. Read it and enjoy the ride!"

> —Karen Duffy, *New York Times* bestselling author of *Backbone*

"A brave, put-your-heart-back-together-again book that's a lesson for all not to hide grief in dark corners, but rather to take it on the open road to celebrate life."

    —Valerie Frankel, author of *The Accidental Virgin*

"Most people would just as soon drown in a pool of grief, self-pity, and tears after the unexpected death of a spouse. Thankfully, Laura Fahrenthold isn't 'most people.' She chose to reframe her remarkable husband's worldly end into a fantastical adventure and beautiful celebration of notable life in a most extraordinary and unconventional way. We should all be so bold."

    —Tara Wood, humor writer

" 'RV there yet?' *The Pink Steering Wheel Chronicles* is the ultimate RV road trip. Reeling from the traumatic death of her beloved husband, journalist Laura Fahrenthold embraces her grief, packs up the kids, a stray dog—and her husband's ashes—and hits the road. Follow Laura's brave, heartwarming, and humorous journey across Canada and beyond, one adventure—and misadventure—at a time. A quintessential tribute to a life well-lived, and a husband well-loved."

    —Sandy Allen, Canadian Blog House

"Laura Fahrenthold takes us on the craziest memorial road trip ever as she scatters her husband's ashes around the country, her two daughters in tow. Her honest, moving, and often hilarious story makes for a sui generis grief memoir that will resonate with anyone who has had to start life over without a map."

    —Julie Metz, author of *Perfection*

"Oh, the comfort that comes from finding a cherished object that belonged to your loved one! Laura Fahrenthold brings readers inside the discovery of her late husband's secret journal, a journey that brings her solace, joy, even much-needed laughter. I found myself staying up way too late to finish this remarkable book."

> —Allison Gilbert, author of *Passed and Present: Keeping Memories of Loved Ones Alive*

"With honesty and intimacy, Laura Fahrenthold recounts her love for her husband and her journey to spread his ashes after his untimely death. She gives parenting a capital 'P' as she teaches her children to adapt both on and off the road."

> —Libby Copeland, journalist for The *Washington Post*, Slate, and Esquire

"Think *Wild* meets *Option B* with each heart thumping mile as this brave widow captains a recreational vehicle she named HaRVey across North America. She becomes the ultimate Girl Scout leader in teaching her daughters (and herself) to rely on their inner strength in navigating everything from mountain tops to changing blown tires.

The Pink Steering Wheel Chronicles will undoubtedly become this year's 'you have to read it' book club choice."

> —Mike McNamara, CEO, Talent Blvd.

The Pink Steering Wheel Chronicles

A Love Story

Laura Fahrenthold

The Pink Steering Wheel Chronicles

Text copyright © 2018 Laura Fahrenthold

Library of Congress Cataloging-in-Publication Data is available upon request.
ISBN: 978-1-57826-768-2

Cover design by Rob Santora, SantoraDesign.com
Interior design by Carolyn Kasper

Printed in the United States
10 9 8 7 6 5 4 3 2 1

Author's Note

This is a work of nonfiction. There are no composite characters, though most names have been changed. As with all memoirs, this story is presented through the lens of my own experience; I have described everything as accurately as I can, to the best of my ability, in the best way that I know how. It is written from the heart.

Dedication

To "Uncle Billy," aka Dr. William Karesh, the
best godfather in the world!

"We are travelers on a cosmic journey,
stardust, swirling and dancing in the eddies
and whirlpools of infinity. Life is eternal.
We have stopped for a moment to encounter
each other, to meet, to love, to share.
This is a precious moment. It is a little
parenthesis in eternity."

—Deepak Chopra

Part I:
I Think I Can,
I Think I Can

1
Out, Out Brief Candle

"I fell to the ground. Blood now pouring
from deep inside my gut as she lay with me,
sweating and soothing my head. It is here
that I lay before the light would shoot me
into the heavens."

—Excerpted from Mark's journals

There are moments we all wish we could have over and over and over again—the moments before everything changes.

I was halfway to the driveway before turning back to kiss Mark goodbye one more time. He called that afternoon to say that he wasn't feeling well and that he was coming home from work early.

"You sure I shouldn't stay home? Maybe you have the flu," I asked, noting the sweat on his pale forehead.

He gave me his sexy lopsided smile, the one that says, "I love you." "I'm fine," he insisted, kissing me back a little *too* passionately for someone with a clammy fever. "We're going to eat a delicious steak dinner, right girls? And then leave for Thanksgiving tomorrow."

"Right, Daddy," echoed Nell and Susannah, happy to have their father all to themselves.

I still can't believe I heard my cell phone ring that night. The restaurant music was really loud, and the place was packed. I can still remember the ringtone: "Piano Riff."

Whenever I hear it now, it makes me want to run out of the room, screaming.

It was Mark. "Laura, help me! I'm throwing up!"

My first thought was that the steak and salad had disagreed with his already upset stomach. But then a surge of lumbering dread shot through me. Mark Pittman never panicked. *Ever.* As a newspaper reporter, he once rushed into a collapsed elementary school to help drag out kids' bodies—some of them dead. Even then, he didn't panic. When covering the September 11th terrorist attacks, he didn't panic. When our newborn baby, Susannah, suddenly stopped breathing after delivery and was rushed off to the neonatal intensive care unit, he didn't panic.

That night, there was something different in his voice. I knew it was an emergency.

The drive home felt like it took forever, even though I only had to blow through five red lights and two stop signs to get there. It was like a slow-motion nightmare where you're running away from something, only your legs won't carry you fast enough.

When I got in the house, Mark burst out of the bathroom, naked, eyes popping wildly as he struggled to compose his body and speech. He staggered, took a few steps, and then fell, gashing his chin on the hallway dresser. Pulling himself up, he collapsed again, this time cutting his forehead. His face bruised almost immediately.

At first, I thought he had been shot or stabbed. There was a lot of blood soaking the piles of clean laundry neatly laid out in preparation for our trip. Some dripped down the wall, puddling on the floor. That's when I realized it was coming out of him, in surges of violent vomit.

For some dumb reason, my first thought was to get him a pair of underwear so that no one would see him naked.

Then came a brutal honking noise. It was coming from Mark, a deep expulsion of air from his lungs. In his hand was a washcloth soaked in blood.

He struggled back to his feet, staggering again and immediately falling face down back on the floor as he collapsed under his own weight. This time, he didn't get up. He didn't move at all.

Then his bladder emptied.

At that exact moment, everything stopped. The air shifted, became lighter. It was almost spotty, like the dots on an old black and white TV. I felt my body being lifted, floating up the attic stairs. I could see us down there, together on the floor, but I was up here, away from us. A gentle rush lifted me even higher, carrying me further away, to some place above. To a higher, sleepy peace. Nothing but blank space swallowing the room in silent calm.

Looking down, I could see myself pressed against him. But up here, I was weightless. Floating in space.

Then, *whoosh*. A noise that sounded like a vacuum cleaner sucked all the air from the room. I was spinning, whirling through muffled space. A hazy gray tunnel with tiny sparkly lights formed in front of me. It got bigger and bigger, gaining power and definition, almost like a tornado's funnel, until it shot straight through the window into the night sky.

Its path was too mesmerizing, the spell too intense to notice that the window had blown wide open as the twinkling trail disintegrated into the star-filled sky. My separation from the tunnel was gentle yet abrupt as the force released me and floated me back down next to him. His body was there, lying still, but he was no longer in it. It was empty.

Mark was gone.

"Mark! Mark! Oh my God! Mark!" I heard myself screaming.

No response.

I checked for breath.

Nothing.

Pulse.

None.

Heartbeat.

Nothing.

Tilt head. Lift chin. Pinch nose. Wipe the blood from his mouth to get a good seal. Give two rescue breaths.

"Come on Mark, breathe!"

No response.

Locate spot where breastbone comes together. Stack hands. Lace fingers together. Okay, GO!

1-2-3-4-5...6-7...8-9-10-11-12...13-14-15...

"Come on, Mark! Can you hear me? If you can hear me, open your eyes! Open your eyes!"

16-17-18...19-20-21...22-23-24-25-26-27...28-29-30...

No response.

Another bloody breath, followed by another. Okay, that's two. Do it again.

1-2-3...4-5-6-7-8-9-10...11-12...

"Oh God! It's going to be okay. I love you! Please, Mark! Breathe for me! You've got to breathe!"

13-14-15-16-17-18-19...

I had forgotten all about the girls. I could hear them crying, calling out to me from behind their bedroom doors.

20-21-22-23-24...

"Do not come out of your rooms! Daddy is sick!" I heard myself saying in that calm yet hysterical voice people use when something really bad is happening. "Go get under your covers and hug your stuffed animals really tight."

25-26...27-28-29-30...

Fill him with breath. Spit the blood out. And again.

"Mark!" Two more breaths.

Barbara had followed me home from the restaurant. By the look on her face, I knew this was bad. Very, very bad. Neither of us spoke. *Maybe if we don't say it, it won't be true.*

"Mrs. Pittman! Listen to me!" the 911 operator called out over the speakerphone. "The ambulance is there. You've got help now. Go to your children. I can hear them crying."

A nice paramedic put a towel over Susannah's head as he carried her from her room to her sister's. He didn't want her to see him stepping over her father's naked body.

He ushered Barbara into the room while instructing me to gather Mark's medications.

Everyone has seen enough TV shows to know what happens next. Paramedics begin rushing in, one of them yelling, "Hand me the paddles!" or "We're losing him!" as alarms start sounding until, miraculously, the machine shocks the patient's heart back to life, saving the day.

What I heard was very different. "No shock advised," the monotone computerized voice called out. In our case, this meant there was no saving the day.

I ran back upstairs, medications in hand, just as they began to inch a plastic tube down his throat. His tongue looked strangely thick and black as it hung from his lips. The paramedic nodded toward Nell's bedroom door, as if to say, "You don't want to be watch this. Go be with your daughters."

The bedroom was pretty much dark except for her blue stained glass nightlight and a ray of moonlight bouncing off the Hudson River. The girls huddled in bed together, clutching each other as they shook under the pink flowered comforter, the one we bought Nell for Christmas the previous year.

"Is Daddy going to die?" Nell whispered, as if her words had the power to make it true.

"Daddy is very, very sick," I told her, "but the ambulance people are doing everything they can to help him. They are going to take him to the hospital, and I need to go hold his hand and make him feel better."

Susannah had started crying really hard now. "Please, Mommy, promise he will get better!"

How do you promise a child something like that? You want to give them hope, to comfort them, but at the same time what if something happens (or perhaps already happened), then what? How can they ever trust your word again?

"The only thing I can promise right now is that no matter what, your father loves you both so, so much, and that I will call you as soon as I can. I have to go help Daddy now. Barbara will stay here with you until I get back."

I grabbed the girls, holding them tight. Nell handed me her teddy bear for a kiss.

"Bye, Delfigalo," I said, pressing my lips against its brown fluffy head.

Susannah's kitty was next.

"Bye Kitty, Kitty Cat. You guys take care of Nell and Susannah, OK?"

What happened to me that night? What was that tunnel, that light? And why did Mark send me back to live life without him?

I've heard of wormholes, where a combination of space and time can connect extremely long distances, billions of light years away across different universes and different points in time. Reflecting back on it now, I wonder if I got caught up in a time travel vortex, as my spirit unknowingly willed itself to follow Mark to the hereafter, or wherever pure hearts and gentle people go. And while the experience may have lasted a mere few seconds, the reality was that it took me the better part of four years to return.

2
DOA

"We are on the eve of death. Hard to tell
when the slide started, but it's been decay
ever since. And now I'm alone. I was alone
yesterday. I'll be alone tomorrow."

—Excerpted from Mark's journals

Mark's friend Billy also raced through red lights to reach the hospital that night. It would be the third time in eight years that he had received "the call." I wondered if he knew that this would be it; if he thought to himself, *Pittman isn't going to make it this time.*

Billy is a doctor, and a former wildlife vet in Africa, so he's someone who can handle these types of out-of-control things. That night in the ER, after putting me in the family waiting room where I was supposed to sit patiently, he spoke with the doctors in that way that doctors do, all hushed and official.

Cracking the door to listen, I heard Billy start to cry.

I'm not sure how anyone expected me to understand without being told outright that meant Mark was gone. Deceased. Not-coming-back-to-life. Instead, I waited. Wasn't someone supposed to burst in to announce that they had miraculously revived him? That he would need a bit of time to recuperate and then he could come home?

I guess I wasn't meant to leave the room, otherwise I would not have found the medics who were *supposed* to be saving him standing there talking and laughing as he lay motionless on the bed.

"What are you doing? This man needs medical attention! You need to revive him! Help him! Fix him! Do something!" I begged.

They just stood there, unable to meet my eyes. Maybe they had been laughing about how hard it was to get the fat bastard off the stretcher and onto the bed. Maybe they were making jokes about the hair on his back or comparing the mole above his left butt cheek to the size of a quarter. I get it, ER humor. But this was *my* husband and that was *our* mole.

"Haven't you read the news reports about the man who came into the hospital dead, but got revived after forty-five minutes of non-stop CPR?" I railed. "You can't give up on your patients like this! What if it were *your* husband or *your* wife lying there?"

They quickly fell back into place, untangling wires and restarting CPR, as a nurse led me back to the padded room. A few minutes later, a doctor appeared, wearing a look of forced sadness on his face.

"Mrs. Pittman," he said as he stood in the doorway, looking a little nervous and distinctly uncomfortable. "Your husband has passed."

"What do you mean, passed?"

"Passed," he repeated.

"Passed? Passed what? Did my husband pass gas? Or are you telling me he's dead? Because if you are telling me he is dead, I am telling you you're *wrong*."

"I'm very sorry. Your husband passed away."

I get that no one wants to do this part of the job, but how difficult would it have been to offer me some sort of lifeline? Something like, "We tried everything possible, every medical treatment known to man." Or, "There were twenty doctors working on him, including Dr. Oz who we flew in via Air Force One to help save your husband. There was nothing more we could do and we are very, very sorry."

I asked for time alone with Mark, expecting to hear no, that it was against hospital rules or something. Instead, a nurse gently held my arm, escorting me back to his room, Trauma E-330.

For some reason, I tiptoed. He looked so sound asleep, I didn't want to wake him.

"Mark, it's me. Are you okay?" I whispered, sticking my finger under his nose to check for breath.

It was so *cold* in there. Bloody tubes protruded from his nose and a spool of wires clung to his chest. The monitors were all turned off.

"You have to wake up now," I sobbed, gently shaking him. Blood began oozing from his nose. "Please wake up, baby. No more stupid doctors. I got rid of them. They're gone. You can get up now. It's over. Time to come home."

No answer.

I lifted his arm into the air. It thudded back down and dangled off the side of the bed.

I pulled his eyelids open: empty brown eyes staring at nothing.

I kissed his lips: they were white and cold.

I held his face in my hands, put my ear to his mouth. He wasn't breathing.

If there was one thing that would wake him up, it was this. Drawing the curtains, I reached for him—down there. His penis lay sleeping on his thigh as I held it in my hand, squeezing it just right. Nothing happened. That's when I knew he was truly dead.

Quietly, secretly, I stripped the wet, bloody clothes from my body and got into bed with him. Positioning his heavy arms around me, I nestled my body against him, resting my head in the exact spot on his chest where it always fit so perfectly. It felt perfect now, too. It was just the two of us, away from all the people and the sirens and the screaming. Calm, alone. Together.

I traced his face with my fingers; his forehead first, then the eyebrows and down to his cheeks. I kissed him all over his beautiful face, like a mother kisses her babies, in tiny white flutters, one after another after another. Head, shoulders, knees, and toes. Eyes and ears and mouth and nose.

It didn't matter to me if anyone could see or hear from the next room or hallway. They couldn't take him away from me. Not yet. We had a lot to talk about, like how I needed him to watch over Nell and Susannah, to guard them and not let anything bad happen to them. He needed to promise to send an angel to take hold of the wheel when they learned to drive. Dislodge a chicken bone from their throats. Pull them up from the bottom of the pool. And for right now, to read them books at night after tucking them into bed.

Wiping away the tears that had splashed down his face and neck, I made promises I knew I could keep—to honor, remember, and to respect him always. To be the best mother I could be. To stand tall, the three of us together, with him and for him.

I'm not sure how long the body keepers let me stay. An hour? Two? But now one of them stood in the doorway, letting me know my time was up. I licked Mark's finger to loosen his wedding band, removing it from his swollen finger before sticking it in my pocket and leaving the room. I did not say goodbye. That's the one thing I refused to say.

I signed the hospital papers, noting how the ER doctor had changed the time of death to 11:59 pm on November 24, instead of dead on arrival, 2:28 am, November 25. Billy told me it was to spare our family from crying in our stuffing for years to come.

Shock. Disbelief. A freezing of emotions.

It felt as though I was following the instructions of an internal voice. Say "thank you" to the nice people, Laura. You need to go home now. Just leave your car in the parking lot and walk; it's only a few blocks away. Clear your head. Lean against a tree. Feel the hard cement on the ground, the cold night air on your face. Search the sky for that gray tunnel with the twinkly lights. Walk past the house. Go around the block. Just keep breathing. Keep walking. Compose yourself.

Then stand there looking back through the window into the dining room. Yes, the table is now empty. And it always will be. It's okay to be afraid you won't make it through the night, much less the rest of your life.

That's where my friend Kim found me. Yes, okay. A shower *is* a good idea. Wedging off my shoes, I held up my arms as she pulled the white ribbed sweater over my head. She unzipped my jeans and tugged them down to my ankles, as I stood shivering on the porch in only my underwear. She cleaned me up with a wet towel before sealing the clothes into a plastic bag. Everything was red.

She did the same to the house, making everything tidy. Stripped the sheets, gathered the blood-soaked piles of laundry, bagged up the syringes, tubes, and gauze left in the hallway. That's what friends do; they spare you the details as you stand in the shower, watching pink water swirl down the drain.

I steadied myself to see my girls. They needed me to be clean and strong, to hold them and kiss their tears.

"Didn't Daddy come home with you?" Susannah asked, her eyes seeping with fear.

How do you say no when you can't believe it yourself?

"He's not coming home," I heard myself say.

Nell pulled the covers down from her face. "Ever?" she whispered, as though saying it any louder would make it real. "You mean forever as in, ever and ever? Or just tonight?"

"Forever...as in forever and ever." I know they will always remember those words when they think about that night, when they play it over and over in their minds like I do.

"I'm so sorry, girls. I am so, so, so sorry."

Keep going, Laura. Don't fall apart. Not now. Don't sugarcoat things by saying God took him, or that he now lives in heaven playing harps with the angels. It would only confuse them more. Best just to say it.

"I have something to tell you that will be very hard to hear," I began, gathering them into my arms, "and that will make you really sad. I have no other way to tell you this. Daddy got very sick and he died tonight."

With those words, I gained a more powerful understanding of what it is to be a mother. It went beyond promising a tiny baby the world. It was just as my own mother would feel as she held me in her arms to make room for my tears.

The girls were too old for baths but wanted to get in the tub together and have me wash their hair like I did when they were little. We formed our famous "pings," when you pull the soapy strands straight up into spikes and look in the hand-held mirror, laughing at the silly hairdos. But there was no laughter tonight; only whimpering and shaking. I tried anyway—tried to go back in time to those lollipop dreams and sticky "I love you" kisses. They held their noses under the faucet to rinse, the magic giggles now gone. I toweled them dry, dressed them in the pajamas Kim had put in the dryer to make all soft and warm, and got in bed with them, picking up where their father had left off in reading *The Golden Compass*. Part Two, Chapter Twelve: "The Lost Boy."

When they eventually fell back to sleep, I lay next to them, silently weeping like the giant willow tree in our backyard.

3

Where Do You Keep the Frying Pans?

"Solitude and silence is often called for when too many questions are asked of the person who doesn't have any answers."

—Excerpted from Mark's journals

Thankfully, Mark's family understood why I didn't want anyone to rush to the rescue.

"I understand, honey," his mom said in her very practical Midwestern way. "There's nothing we can do now anyway. You take care of yourself and the girls. We'll come in a few days."

My mother would not take no for an answer. When she found she couldn't get on the next flight out, she began packing up the car to drive—all the way from North Carolina to New York.

"Mom's on her way to your house," my sister, Wendy, called to tell me.

"Make her turn around, Wendy. Tell her no. I need time. I can't handle this. Not yet. Not now."

Everything could wait until Monday. I needed time alone to think. To process. But even as I sagged down onto the couch, I realized it was useless. First my mom would be here, and then...everyone. The house would fill up with people crying in the living room until it was time to cook a meal. And then I'd end up taking my stress out on them, when all they were doing was trying to be kind and helpful.

"Where do you keep the frying pans?" they'd ask.

Look on the hanging pot rack right there above your head.

"Do you have any salt? And flour?"

The spices and baking supplies are in the cabinet next to the stove on the left. No, the second shelf.

"Are the eggs fresh?"

Yes. That's why there are four chickens in the backyard. To lay fresh eggs every day.

After battering the fish in flour, fresh eggs, and salt, then frying it, everyone would sit down to an awkward meal where even small talk seemed inappropriately out of place. We would then eat in silence, watching the clock tick on the wall, until finally the dog scratched his head and the clank of his collar tags would somehow kick off a conversation about bed bug infestations, especially at nice hotels. The mundanity of conversation would be too much for...someone, perhaps Mark's father, who would then politely excuse himself from the table to go upstairs where no one would hear him sobbing into a pillow.

The families would soon ask if they could go through Mark's things, to take something that reminded them of him. Albums, clothes, or, *if I wouldn't mind*, perhaps his Hunter Thompson book collection?

Right now, all I wanted was to bolt the doors on our lives. Everything he touched had become sacred; nothing was to move an inch.

"Please don't take his coat off the chair," I would say, feeling panicky whenever someone entered a room. "That's exactly where he left it."

"Please don't put his newspapers in the recycling bin. Those were the last words he read."

"Please don't remove his half-empty water glass from the nightstand. I'll just...let it evaporate."

Family and friends would need to enter the Mark Pittman Hall of Fame at their own risk.

At night, my mother would want to sleep in our giant king-sized bed with me. But I didn't want her to, because then the pillows wouldn't smell as much like Mark anymore. I needed them to smell like him as much as possible and for as long as possible. Still, I needed her to comfort me, to fill that empty space and to hold me each night until I cried myself to sleep, the same as I did for my own daughters.

4

What Is Past
Is Prologue

"Talking to the stars. That's what it's all
about. It's the only time they can hear you
when it's dark and you're alone. That's
when the one-on-one work gets done, not in
the force of fits and starts. It's when you
gently surrender to the Amen."

—Excerpted from Mark's journals

They say your life flashes before your eyes when you die, and I
now know why. Alone at night, I would stare out the window
looking to the stars as the chapters of our lives replayed themselves,
like the pages of his long-forgotten journal being wind-whipped down
the street.

It was five years after Mark's death that I found a green folder
labeled: "Mark's writings." *That's strange*, I thought. *How could I have
missed this?* We had shared a desk and filing system for fifteen years.
Yet there they were, thirty-five double-spaced typewritten pages;
dispatches from a long-haired motorcycle trip he took back in the 70s.

The more I read, the more I heard his whisper in my ear. The sensation was both warm and eerie, filling me with cosmic context—even more than the sunflower did.

That's when I called the most sane person I know.

"I'm not sure I believe in reincarnation or an afterlife or heaven or hell or any of that stuff, but what do you think of this?" I began breathlessly after my step-father answered.

Some sections narrated the exact same emotions I had been experiencing. Others detailed several of the remote places that the girls and I inexplicably felt drawn to.

But then, there were the parts about Samuel, a fictional character he created whose death exactly mirrored his own. It was as if Mark had already lived a previous life, or lives.

The writings revealed moments in parallel, describing many of the places the girls and I visited in the years following his death where I felt him suddenly appear by our sides, as though to walk with us or to lead us.

It was this presence that propelled me to ignore all warnings and drive through wildfire areas to get to Sedona. And now, could it have possibly been Mark who guided me to drive for sixteen hours straight to visit his father and stepmother-in-law? Her cancer diagnosis came just a few days after we left.

I could hear tears in George's voice. The only time I'd ever seen him cry was at Mark's funeral. "Honey," he said, "I remember all of it. I didn't know how to comfort you then, and not now, either. Maybe these are just incredible coincidences?"

That's why I had waited to tell him the rest—the parts about "Samuel," who plowed fields as a homesteader in Kansas back in the 1860s. He had a wife, Ruth, two unnamed daughters, and a son called Isaac. They prayed a lot, which I guess is what you do when you don't know if the rains will come.

"Mark wrote about Samuel collapsing and vomiting blood and dying. The details, the way he described it...was exactly the same as his own death," I told George.

"Read it to me."

```
Specks of blood filled my handkerchief. By
then, it was pouring from me. A river of
blood. I see it coming. And it passes through
me: a speeding, blinding light. It carries
me to the heavens. Everything changed in a
shooting flash.
```

We were both thinking the same thing: about how I found Mark holding a handkerchief spotted with blood before it started pouring out of him, too. And how I saw the flash and *felt* that shooting tunnel lifting us up the attic stairs.

"Listen to this," I continued after a moment, reminding him how Mark had fallen and how his face bruised. "'*How long will it take before I collapse of my own weight? My body screams, bruises forming.*' And from there, it's almost a flash-forward to him describing the CPR. '*She paused for breath and took another and another. Her breath was my life, but I was slipping, and I knew it.*'"

I continued before he could possibly interrupt. "Did I ever tell you how Mark's tongue turned black when he died? I don't mean to be gross, but it did. Mark wrote about that, too.

'*In my sleep, my tongue is black,*' he said."

The more we discussed his "writings," the more convinced we became that Mark may have already lived another man's life, and possibly his own, too.

The journals explained so much. They helped me to make sense of...everything, really.

It wasn't until now—years later—that I realized it didn't matter how far I traveled or how hard I pushed myself in between, I had to learn to live with the void.

And while I thought his death was the greatest loss I could ever suffer, I also realized that the greatest loss is what dies inside of us as we continue to live.

That's why you can never really say goodbye. It's why, to this day, I still find myself searching for his face in crowds of people.

This is my story...

5

When Lois Met Clark

"Today's my lucky day. She walked in and stood before me, blue eyes looking into mine. I'm not a praying man, but I'd get down on my knee, asking for her love. If she motioned to the floor, there I would lay to be with her."

—Excerpted from Mark's journals

There once lived a boy named James Mark Pittman, the story begins. His mother was just sixteen when she gave birth to him—the first of three sons—in Kansas City, Kansas.

Back then, when the knee of your Wrangler jeans wore out, your mom ironed on a denim patch, then sewed it good and tight. You rode your red Schwinn bike to school, mowed your grandmother's yard or shoveled her driveway on Sundays after church, and always did what your daddy told you.

Without knowing it, Mark's journalism career began at around age thirteen. Hiding under his bed covers with a flashlight and pen in hand, he would stay up writing political stories for the school newspaper, stories about Vietnam, napalm bombs, communism, and Watergate.

Five years of (almost) straight A's later, Harvard wanted to recruit Mark, but he needed to continue working alongside his father at the Piggly Wiggly grocery store. He eventually transferred from a junior college to Kansas University for in-state tuition, first in the engineering program, but he quickly switched to journalism. His home was an abandoned building where he lived with a few other cash-strapped friends, surviving on beer, Marlboros, Cheerios, and Bob Dylan.

At one point, he took a part-time job as a ranch hand across the border in Lenapah, Oklahoma. That's where he wore the cowboy boots I loved so much. And the hat; it's up on the bookshelf now, resting atop the black box that holds his ashes. It's dusty, the hat, but I like it all worn out like that.

Mark would soon discover Hunter Thompson, the legendary writer who branded "Gonzo" journalism, a methodology where reporters involve themselves in the action to such a degree that they become the central figures of their stories. "Hell's Angels: The Strange and Terrible Saga of the Outlaw Motorcycle Gangs" was possibly his favorite. Thompson spent that writing year riding with the Hell's Angels, experiencing their lives and hearing their stories first-hand. Both men reveled in a love of freedom and an iconoclastic contempt for authoritarianism.

"Cool," I could almost hear Mark say when deciding to turn in his cowboy hat for a motorcycle helmet one college summer while in search of his own gonzo experiences.

He always went for the underbelly.

"That's where the real stories are, not in the ivory towers," he would say. This was long before he began investigating the U.S.

federal government to discover it was hiding one of the biggest secrets in American history.

First, he did what you're "supposed to do:" graduate college, get a good job (in his case, at a small regional newspaper, the Coffeyville Journal), marry your college sweetheart, have a beautiful baby. Maybe buy a house someday.

Problem was, Mark still had Hunter Thompson and motorcycle oil in his blood. He was restless—bored with small town Kansas life. He wanted to break "major ass" stories, not cover village hall meetings. He soon left Kansas for a new job in Rochester, New York, covering the cop beat at the *Democrat & Chronicle*. Even though he was now in my hometown and we lived close enough to see each other's roofs (if you stood all the way to the left of my front porch and squeezed your head against the side of the house), it would still be ten years before we would meet.

I had moved to Boston for my first job as assistant editor of a regional magazine. But within a few years, the bright lights of New York began calling, and I used the last of my paychecks to rent the cheapest apartment I could find in the safest neighborhood I could find—a $450 a month, sixth-floor, 102-step walk-up studio on E. 80th between 2nd and 3rd, complete with a claw foot bathtub in the kitchen and a toilet in the common hallway. After a few months of job hunting while surviving on $4 a day, I got a job. And not just any job, a real journalism job at a *real* New York City newspaper! Sure, it was answering the news tip phone lines, but it was still at the *New York Daily News*. It got me in the door, which was all that mattered. Soon after, I was offered the position of crime reporter at the "the cop shop," better known as police headquarters in lower Manhattan.

Meanwhile, Mark had left his reporter's job in Rochester to become metro editor at the *Times-Herald Record* in Middletown, New York, about sixty miles out of the city. It's where he stayed for more than a decade: loving his job, enjoying his family, and drinking beer

with his buddies after Friday night baseball. Everything was fine...
until his wife asked for a divorce.

Not long after, in walks this girl, a new Sunday features writer.
After six years, I had burned out on city life and wanted nothing more
than to work at a smaller paper and live in a lakefront cabin.

It was a move that changed both of our lives.

It was my first day, and here was this big, tall, incredibly handsome
man with worn cowboy boots propped up on a desk, commanding
two phones at once while punching notes into the computer keyboard,
a line of reporters waiting to talk with him. He was taking it all in,
laughing and joking around, even on deadline. This guy was, in three
words, larger-than-life.

When his hand went out to shake mine, everything stopped—
including my heart.

"Hi, I'm Mark Pittman." He stood up, smiling that incredible
smile at me.

I wasn't sure what my name was for a moment, but I was sure I
wanted him to know it.

"Laura...Laura Fahrenthold," I managed, extending my own hand.
He held my eyes, never looking away. Neither could I.

That's when I knew he would end up being the most important
person in my life.

My first lead story came out of a small Dairy Queen town while
covering an extra night shift on the police beat.

"Hi, it's the *Times-Herald Record*. Anything going on tonight?" I
had to call up each station on the checklist, looking for news tips. The
desk cops' answers were typically, "Nope. All's quiet here."

But something told me things *weren't* quiet when I heard the Village of Maybrook officer suck in his breath. That meant he was holding something back.

Mark always said cop reporters end up with "big BS detectors" because everyone lies to you. "The cops lie to you, the victims lie to you, the people helping the victims lie to you. And you've got to sort through it all," he'd tell people. "The story that seems a certain way just won't be—and you know it."

Turns out, the officer wasn't just lying, he was covering up that a twelve-year-old boy, Danny Meyer, had been found stabbed to death in the woods while walking home from Little League practice. At first, police suspected one of the transient carnival workers from the weekend fair. One team worked that angle with state police while another retraced Danny's day, including his last steps in the woods.

That's where a boy, Juan Peinado, was found hanging from a tree with a noose around his neck, bicycle below his feet. The photographer managed to cut him down with a pocketknife, rushing him to the police station where the boy gave a detailed account of being attacked by a man in a black hoodie. At the same time, a police source informed me that Danny had been sodomized in an act of necrophilia. I called it into the newsroom. Was Juan Peinado sodomized, too?

Within a nanosecond, the sky was filled with a swirl of helicopters as news trucks and reporters surrounded the tiny village, population 2,958. It was like the O.J. Simpson trial; news became entertainment as people camped out on picnic blankets with pizza deliveries to stay on top of the action.

Mark and I didn't believe Juan's story from the start. Eventually, he confessed. He was Danny Meyers' killer and had faked his own attack in hopes of throwing the police off.

Night after night, we stayed late in the newsroom or went to the local diner to discuss the case until we discovered, through visitor records, that the only person to visit Juan in jail was a priest. More hunches and a few weeks of leads later, we learned Juan had come to America from Guatemala as a foster child. Not only that, but he was twenty-one, not sixteen as his paperwork stated. More digging led us to believe he was really part of a sex ring and had finally snapped as a result of the abuse. But there was no way to prove it without going to Guatemala.

Case closed, but never forgotten. To this day, I still worry and pray for Danny's parents.

Meanwhile, Mark and I had fallen madly in love. And when he got down on one knee with sunflower in hand to propose that we get married, I was never so sure of anything in my life.

He always surprised me with sunflowers—in my car, under my pillow, in the blue vase on the table. Whenever I see one now, I go back to the bright summer day when he led me, blindfolded, into a giant field of buttery Kansas sunflowers after taking me home to meet his family. It was one of the most beautiful things I had ever seen, so many flowers at once. He spread a blanket in a clearing on the ground and we lay in that field, looking up at the tall stalks of yellow leaves overhead in the vast blue sky, knowing that we had found our own special heaven. He would often sing, "You are my sunflower, my only sunflower," to wake me up in the morning, which annoyed me as often as it made me laugh, but it always filled me with complete love.

Still, the deepest part of me worried about being responsible for another human being, much less be married to one and possibly having kids with one. What if it all went wrong, the way so many marriages do? Then what? Worse, what if he left me for another woman, like my father had done to my mother?

Couldn't we just stay living together? Or better yet, couldn't we live in separate apartments in the same building? That way, we wouldn't wear out our relationship. Or, how about a commitment ceremony rather than an official wedding?

"Relax, babe," he said with amusement while holding my chin in place, so I would have to look at him in the eyes without squirming away. "My purpose in life—it's to love you."

"You say that now but look at what happens to people. What if it happens to us?"

"Shh..." he would whisper, cutting me off. "I promise I will never leave you. I promise I will never hurt you or cheat on you or lie to you or abandon you or our children."

"What children? You're pregnant?"

I liked it that he laughed at my bad jokes.

"The children we are we are going to have," he said. "I see girls. Two of them. Maybe we can name one of them Ruth? For some reason, I've always felt connected to that name."

And I felt connected to Mark. He calmed me in the deepest, most settled of ways. And that made all the difference.

We excitedly set out with new jobs and a move back to the city. He would now cover the financial markets at Bloomberg News, and I went to work as a features editor at Woman's World Magazine. We moved to Carroll Gardens, Brooklyn.

He wanted to get "properly" married in a church. *In a white dress with vows and everything?* I thought. *Really?* We did—we got married in a beautiful, old stone church and held a picnic reception at the Saugerties Lighthouse on the Hudson River.

Next when he wanted to get started on a family for real, I worried. *Me? A mother?* I couldn't imagine being a mother. I didn't want to be a mother. The thought of it literally terrified me. But just four months later, I was so excited to be pregnant with Nell, and four months after welcoming her to the world, our plan worked. We were pregnant again.

With our second child on the way, it was time to say goodbye to our tiny apartment and city life. We bought a modest house just north of the city, in Yonkers, and moved just two months before Susannah was born.

It was hectic and crazy and wonderful. I couldn't believe how much our love had grown, that there were even deeper layers to the levels. Any honest couple will say the same thing: relationships and marriage can be hard at times, even when you love the person so much you can't imagine how you lived without them. But it goes way beyond wet towels on the floor or budgeting to replace the cracked driveway. It's the modern-day problem—two people balancing their careers with home life.

I was lucky to be able to do both by working at home, raising the girls while earning a living in a career that I loved. It wasn't that Mark didn't *want* to leave work at 5:00 pm to make it home in time for dinner, baths, pajamas, and books; it's that he often had to work later and longer to cover whatever the big news story was of the day, or produce what's called an enterprise piece, a story that a reporter digs up on his or her own that goes beyond covering events, news conferences, and press releases. He often spent parts of the weekend working from home, too.

I'll admit that it sometimes made me want to run back to my carefree, single life—the one I had before, where I had been free to do what I wanted, when I wanted and how I wanted. No husband, no children, no mortgage; and while I was so in love with him and so proud of him and so happy with our lives, I sometimes found myself resenting him for giving me everything I never knew I wanted.

But then all that lamenting would fly out of my mind and I'd worry as I watched him sleeping on the couch, exhausted and puffy-eyed. *This pace can't last,* a little voice warned me. Whose voice was that? Mine? The doctor's?

6

I'm Fine

"Emotion. What the hell do I feel? Rage, pain of parting? Nah, just a sort of existential despair that I wake with every morning knowing that the end is one less day away. I hide it well. She knows little of my fears."

—Excerpted from Mark's journals

A heart attack? Are you kidding me? How is it even possible that a forty-two-year old even have a heart attack? We were so naïve.

He had gone to a concert with Billy after work but left during intermission. He was having a hard time breathing and blamed it on allergies, despite never having been allergic to anything before. By morning, I knew something was terribly wrong. His face was pale and gray.

At first, he refused to go to the hospital. No one goes to the ER for a little asthma, especially on Father's Day.

"Too bad," I told him. "We're going!"

"Really, I'm fine. Don't worry!" he said waving me off from the ER waiting room so I could go home to feed Susannah rather than having a family member bring her to us. She was only two months old. "I'll be here for hours before they even call my name anyway. Take your time."

Just then, the doctor called us into the exam room. An EKG and blood test followed, confirming the doctor's suspicion that Mark had suffered a heart attack. They could stabilize him with IV medication while I went home to get the baby, but he would be going to Columbia Presbyterian Hospital's Rusk Heart Institute—by ambulance—for further testing.

He needed stents—two of them—to open the blockages that caused the lack of blood flow to the heart in the first place.

His regular doctor was calling it a "mild" heart attack. Routine stuff, really. He needed to eat better. Get more exercise. Sleep more. Blah, blah. What he didn't say is Mark was twenty-four years younger than the average male heart attack victim and that we should be worried, very worried.

A few years later, he fell while walking across the street, breaking his ankle in six places. It took four metal plates, eight screws, and a piece of his hip bone to fuse the bones back together, not to mention six weeks recuperation and follow up knee surgery. It didn't occur to me until later that the doctor should have questioned what caused him to fall on dry pavement in the first place.

Six more years passed before he was rushed to hospital again for emergency stent surgery. This time, he failed a routine angiogram— the one I insisted he get after noticing his face turning that purple gray color again.

The hospital surgeon gave me a very different prognosis than the one I had received from Mark's regular doctor.

"Mrs. Pittman," he called out into the waiting room.

I turned to look for Mark's mother, until I realized he was speaking to me (I *was* Mrs. Pittman).

"I have no other way to say this," he began. "Your husband needed three more stents, and there is evidence of massive heart disease..." He took a measured pause, placing his hands on my shoulders before delivering the next part. "I don't know how to tell you this, but he will be lucky to live another two to three years. Four, tops," he said, pointing to the x-ray pinned to a light box on the wall. It showed a snarl of veins and arteries. You didn't need to be a doctor to know that it looked bad—very bad. His beautiful heart looked like it had a ball of yarn rewound around it by a two-year-old.

"You need to enjoy your lives together now, every day," he said with total sincerity. He was visibly upset. Heartbroken, really. "I'm so sorry. I know how hard this is to hear. It's not fair, I know," he said, soothing me as I wept, whereas Mark's doctor left me twitching in the hallway.

I can recite that second conversation verbatim, as well as the one that followed. Some things never leave you.

"You want me to send him to the Pritikin *what*?" Mark's doctor almost demanded, his voice a terse whisper as we stood outside the hospital room.

"The Pritikin Center," I repeated. "It's a highly-recommended, healthy lifestyle change program in Florida." I had done my research. "It looks ideal for someone like Mark. He can recharge, take meditation and wellness classes, eat healthy meals, and go on a physician-supervised cardiac exercise program."

Maybe he could live a few extra years. Maybe by then they'll be able to fix his heart and he can live forever.

Crossing his arms defensively, he told me he couldn't write that prescription *or* make that recommendation.

"Why not?" I insisted.

He returned that he could not "in good conscience" send my husband anywhere for a month. He acted as though I were asking for an exotic vacation to a Tiki hut resort in Southeast Asia or something. I was not suggesting that anyone "give him a month off work;" I was simply suggesting that he do what doctors are supposed to do—anything and everything to help save someone's life. But if you asked Mark, he insisted to the doctor and to me and to everyone around him that he was "fine."

I still wonder: would life have turned out differently otherwise?

7

The Revolution
Starts Now

"You go and burn my crops and my neighbor's
crops? For your own survival? Time for
business, boys. Quiet deliberation is the
only way to win a war."

—Excerpted from Mark's journals

Every time he was a little late coming home from work, I imagined him riding dead on the train, slumped in a cracked hard-shell plastic subway seat while commuters pushed past his limp legs, thinking how tired that poor guy must be to sleep so heavily. Or if he took "too long" running a weekend errand, I paced at the door, waiting to hear his Dodge Durango pull in the driveway.

I played the innocent teenager whose parents had come home unexpectedly.

"Oh, nothing," I would say casually over my shoulder when he asked what I was doing.

Like a good soldier's wife, I knew the doorbell could ring any day; the police wouldn't have to say a word as they stood there on the step, looking uncomfortably down at their feet.

Of course, death could also come at home. During a longer-than-usual nap, I caught myself tiptoeing into the room to watch his back for signs of movement and to hold my hand in front of his face to feel his breath. Sometimes, if my finger accidentally grazed his nose, he would startle awake.

"For God's sake, Laura," he would snort. "I'm *fine*."

He never acknowledged what the surgeon had told me. "You must have misunderstood that guy," he insisted. "My doctor said I just need to take my cholesterol pills, go to the gym more, and get more sleep. I feel great. Really, I do."

But he didn't look it. Or act it. This led to some major arguments where he insisted the surgeon was wrong and I insisted Mark was ignoring his health.

"Oh, Laura," he would say in that exasperated tone he used when he had enough of me. "I'm better now. Look at me, babe. Everything's going to be fine."

"Don't call me babe," I'd shoot back. "How can you possibly say you're fine when your face is all pale and gray? You're exhausted. Admit it—you're *sick*. No doctor would say that to me otherwise, even yours."

The arguments typically ended the same way. I would beg him to quit his job, move to the country, become a lumberjack. Or maybe we could farm lettuce. That would be "fine." No? Could he at least work from home a few days a week?

His placating was so masterful that I often fell for it when he would promise, with cheerful sincerity, to think about it...once he got through with whatever the big story was at the time.

None of his dedication had to do with earning capacity, either. He got paid the same whether he worked eight hours or twelve. Mark was caught between his two great loves; he prided himself on our family life, but every part of him *lived* for breaking news.

He regularly came home telling me about whatever big financial story he was onto. Only now it was something *really, really* big. (*Blah, blah,* subprime mortgage housing crisis, I can't hear anything else, *blah, boring,* the government and the banks are doing something with taxpayers' money to cover up a recession, if not a depression, *yeah, okay.*)

The entire U.S. economy might collapse? Within six months? Okay, Mark, whatever you say. Let's just have a nice dinner.

Six months later, the stock market crashed.

But at that moment, I didn't care about America or banks or even having to stand in a bread line. All I cared about was him.

The thing is, he wasn't a wired adrenaline junkie or the loud, obnoxious, stressed-out type. He was cooler than that. Like his colleague Ryan Chittum said, Mark Pittman had fire; he had guts. He was six feet four, and self-assured. Not smug; he was simply fearless. He believed that his purpose was to bring difficult truths to light. He wanted to find out what was wrong in the world, to name names and right social injustices. He was known as the "moral force" of the newsroom. He never met an official whose story he didn't question, a lead he didn't follow, or a wall he didn't bulldoze in pursuit of truth. There was no "thin line" between wrong and right with him. If he said it, he meant it. And if he made a promise, he kept it.

He carried with him a Midwestern union-worker's son's I ain't "impressed" attitude toward his Wall Street beat and its trappings of intellectual superiority. That's one reason why he got the stories that broke vital information and changed the public conversation. People trusted him with their truths, both in the glass skyscrapers and at the gas pump. The guy was a magnet.

Soon after starting at Bloomberg, he was going after the most powerful institutions in the world. Goldman Sachs? Why not? The Fed? Who the hell else? He became Bloomberg's bulldog, the guy manning the con when things started going wild on Wall Street.

Lenders began giving out mortgages to anyone with a pulse, regardless of their ability to handle the loan—loans which kicked in at ridiculously high interest rates upwards of twenty-four percent in a lot of cases after the teaser rate period ended. Soon, people (typically poor people with no resources) were unable to repay and started losing, and often abandoning, their homes. But many lenders didn't care. All they wanted was the initial money—lots and lots of it.

Mark suspected the Federal Reserve was pumping money not only into the banks, but into other financial institutions like Lehman Brothers, who declared bankruptcy before the effects of the world financial crisis could seep into ordinary people's daily lives. What's more, not only was this information being withheld from the public, taxpayers were paying for it. The Feds would not disclose which banks, if any, were borrowing money or how much they needed to avoid running out of money and shutting down, causing a mass panic among the American people.

Imagine going to the bank and having them tell you, "Sorry, you can't have any money. We're closed. Your money's all gone. We spent it. Have a nice day."

Mark filed a Freedom of Information Act request in order to blow the lid off the banking system and the corruption behind it. This law gives citizens, including journalists, a way to shake unpleasant information from the government. It also gives the government a way to say no, which is what the Fed did. They effectively told Mark to stuff it.

One thing you don't do is tell Pittman to stuff anything—especially when it came to keeping someone from getting "screwed over."

He came home that night telling me, "The revolution starts now!"

That's the way Mark was: he had great concern for the "everyman." It's what drove him. "Speculation is an American thing, and we like that," he explained. "We're a gambling people, which is okay...but where it impacts regular folks, you have to *do* something about it. You've got to rein it in a bit; make sure the rules are fair."

Mark wasn't about to give up. But at this point, the only way for him to pursue the data now was to sue the Federal Reserve, the most powerful financial institution in the world. This was supported by Michael Bloomberg, the billionaire owner of Bloomberg News.

"Go for it," Bloomberg said.

And that's how Mark became the only reporter on the planet to sue the Fed.

8

Against the Wind

"Sometimes it was better not to say anything;
to let her think it was a derivative of her
mind rather than the reality or the truth.
It was me against the wind and I was fighting
for breath."

—Excerpted from Mark's journals

Did I really want Mark to walk away from the biggest story of his life?

Yes, yes, yes. And yes. A thousand, hundred, million, trillion times, *yes*. By this time, his team at work began winning all kinds of national journalism awards, including the Loeb Award for a five-part series on the origins of the crisis called "Wall Street's Faustian Bargain." It featured his lead story on how the Street goosed the subprime mortgage market with financial engineering. They received two Pulitzer Prize nominations. His work drew the attention of filmmakers Andrew and Leslie Cockburn, who prominently featured him in *American Casino*, a documentary about the collapse of the subprime mortgage market.

Was the housing crisis or recession or depression or banking emergency and eventual stock market crash more important than his health? And what about us?

The daily stress of watching his health unfold manifested itself into my having full blown panic attacks where my teeth chattered uncontrollably, my body convulsing like a wet dog pulled from an icy pond. Mark would literally have to lay his entire body on top of me to stop the shaking as he stroked my hair, wet with sweat, and kissed my forehead and face, all while promising over and over again not to die.

Sometimes I almost believed it. But then I'd hear his heavy breathing as he climbed the stairs or catch sight of his face turning that awful purplish-grey. And I'd worry. It was hard not to get mad after finding him sitting at his computer at 2 am, pounding away on the keyboard talking to reporters in other time zones like Hong Kong or London.

"They're not going to change your name from Mark Pittman to Mark Bloomberg on your gravestone," I snapped. I hated it when I spoke to him like that but hoped that being brutally blunt might have more of an impact than honey sweet (though I had tried that, too).

We learned the hard way that not having life insurance even at our young ages was an oversight. And there was now no hope of getting it without paying ten times the price. I later learned he had been quietly putting a little extra toward our mortgage payments each month—anything to help us get by a little easier without him.

For fun, he got a new grill, all the while enjoying his steaks washed down with big California reds. On weekends, we threw regular dinner parties, filling the house with friends. He got tickets to the Metropolitan opera. He spent hours playing ballerina and having tea parties with the girls, dressing up the dog and once painting his toenails red (much to the girls' delight). He began baking desserts with the girls—key lime pie and chocolate mousse were their favorites.

And at night, after tucking them into bed, he would reach for me even more than ever before.

Sometimes, I would work myself into heaving sobs as if he really *had* died, and rehearse how to break it to his mother.

"Donna, Mark is dead."

But no, that was way too abrupt. I needed to lean into it more.

"Donna, it's Laura. I have very bad news. Can you sit down?"

But bad news could mean anything from another terrorist attack to something happening to her granddaughters—perhaps while he was driving. Then she would have a heart attack and that would mean more phone calls.

"Donna. It's Laura. Mark had another heart attack, only this time he didn't make it. Donna, he's gone," I'd say, imagining her shock and the unendurable pain a mother would feel upon hearing that her child had died.

All of this made me cry impossibly harder, especially when I brought our children and other family members into the storyline.

"What is wrong with me?" I asked Amy, my therapist. Amy had been seeing me on and off since Mark's first heart attack, and had helped me through the high alerts, my panic attacks, and other assorted matters of life. Her office had become a refuge of sorts, though I wasn't much comforted by the space. Do people really lay down on that ugly leather couch, I wondered? It's so cliché, really, to have a couch in a therapist's office. I always took the red chair: the proverbial hot seat.

Amy told me that it's completely normal to create these doom and gloom fantasies, that it was the mind's way of coping with stress—something she called "anticipatory grief."

If I was so textbook normal, then why I was paying her to "therapy" me?

To this day, I still can't remember whether I called Donna or she called me.

9

Death Takes No Holidays

"As I pull the knife slowly out of my chest,
where it slides off ribs between muscles,
I stare at my assailant with eyes that are
starting to fill with tears."

—Excerpted from Mark's journals

The phone call I do remember came a few hours after he died, on Thanksgiving, when most everyone in the country was about to sit down to their turkey dinners. It was a nice lady at the hospital, asking politely if they could carve Mark.

Kim was fielding all calls. "Uh huh. Okay. Yes, she's right here. Hold on, please."

"It's the hospital," she whispered, covering the mouthpiece. "They're calling to talk to you about organ donation."

Don't misunderstand: organ donation is a good thing. It's just that I didn't expect the call. The woman's voice carried that monotone yet singsong quality, that sort of focus group-tested neutral tone that says, "I was trained to speak to bereaved families in a way that won't offend them, but will also make them feel really guilty for saying no."

I think that's what made me be rude to the angel of death. Whoops. I mean the angel of life, of course.

"You want whose organs? Mark Pittman's organs? You're joking, right?" *Didn't they know about my husband's love of red meat, cigars, wine, and whiskey? And weren't his organs too old, anyway?"*

The woman politely clarified that only his skin and corneas qualified.

It was the same initial reaction I had at the hospital when they told me he needed an autopsy. Hadn't he been through enough for one day? But it's state law whenever a person dies an "unattended" death, meaning when they don't die in the hospital.

I didn't *want* to think about what was going to happen next even though I *knew* what was going to happen next.

First, they would make a U-shaped incision running from his shoulders down. Then everything from the adrenal glands to the reproductive organ would get cut out. (Really? Did they really have to cut *that?*)

Oh, and next would be the brain, which would be removed by cutting his head open in the back of the skull and slitting it from one ear to the other. The scalp would then get separated from the underlying skull and pulled forward. Then they'd take a saw to the top of his skull and "gently" lift the brain out of the cranial vault. (What's the point of gently lifting out someone's brain after you just brutally sawed their head open?)

After laying out all of his organs laid out on the table, tissue samples would be taken to pathology before sewing him up. Good as new.

10

Ashes to Go, Please

"I long now for calm radiant confidence, for
garland and soothing comfort: a cool hand
laid upon my sweating brow, as I look into
the fire that burns before me."

—Excerpted from Mark's journals

There was never any question of what to do with his body. Mark wanted to be cremated.

While that seemed straightforward enough, I found myself getting sidetracked by researching the environmental toll of traditional burials. I estimated that each year nearly thirty million square feet of hardwood is used to create caskets in North America alone. That's enough wood to frame more than 2,300 single-family homes. And get this: more than 100,000 tons of steel is used to make caskets and vaults. Think fifteen Eiffel Towers per year. And that doesn't include the more than sixteen million tons of concrete used to reinforce the burial vaults, almost four times as much concrete as was used to build the Pentagon. And we mustn't forget the eight Olympic-size swimming pools worth of embalming fluid used every year—an estimated 827,060 gallons.

Even putting aside all the resources that burials take, I couldn't stand the thought of him slowly rotting away underground somewhere, trapped for all eternity.

Come to find out, cremation wasn't as simple as it seemed, either.

"Hello, McMahon's funeral home. How may I help you?"

No, I *didn't* want to accompany Mark's body to their "Where Memories Live Forever" chapel for a ten-minute service before they turned him to ash. I never wanted to see him dead again or watch an attendant wheel his body (carefully packaged in a box marked "head first") into the incineration room to be roasted at 1400–1800, where he would lay for almost three hours while some sallow-faced worker sat marveling at the size of his body before transferring his bones into the pulverizing machine.

"Hey, Joe! Get a load of this one," the ash collector would say. "Must've been a big dude."

"Holy guacamole! Look at the size of his bones," I could hear them joking.

Then the kindly funeral home director would hand me a pamphlet about "personal emotional journeys" before proceeding with a lot of questions.

Did I want a memorial or columbarium niche? The first is where they put the urn in a glass viewing display case, like a protected museum artifact; the second has the urn sealed in a series of niches carved into the walls of a mausoleum. Then you choose the style: glass, bronze, or marble front.

The price? It was like premium shelf space at the Piggly Wiggly: $900 to be at the very top where no one could see him alongside the generic brand sauces; $10,000 to place him at eye level in one of those premium spots where the Ragu and the Prego would sit; $1,800 and down at the bottom with the Chef Boyardee.

But wait, there's more! A name inscription and interment would be an additional $600. Or, if I was looking for a bargain and didn't mind the idea of tossing my loved one in the sale cart with the expired vitamins and oddly-flavored vinegars, I could opt to "commingle" his ashes in a deep hole with other people's cremains, consigning my husband to the crematorium version of a mass grave for a mere $525. Finally, for those doomsday preppers who see all bunker rations as equal, there was the permanent storage option (aka the basement) with no nameplate (because no one would see him anyway, so who cares) for *only* $429.

"At least there, you can retrieve them if you have to," offered the funeral home's salesman of the year.

There was no way I'd do any of this, especially locking my husband up in a marble echo chamber where the only thing to break the silence is the sound of heels, whispers, and weeping. Otherwise, it's stone quiet in there.

In the end, I asked for his ashes to go. There was no way I would leave him there all by himself, whether his roommate was a chef or not. Thanks, but no thanks.

11

Extra, Extra, Read All About... The Conspiracy!

"All thoughts become issues when mired in
belief that nothing happens by accident,
nothing is as it seems, and everything
is connected. There is no way of knowing
the truth now, only the facts between the
suspension of their reality."

—Excerpted from Mark's journals

I can now recite the Bloomberg News obituary word for word after reading it over and over. Seeing it in print somehow made it more real, more believable.

"Mark Pittman, the award-winning reporter whose fight to make the Federal Reserve more accountable to taxpayers led Bloomberg News to sue the central bank and win, died Nov. 25, 2009 in Yonkers, New York. He was 52."

It struck me most that Mark was born on the 25th of October and died on the 25th of November at age 52. What was it with him and the numbers 2 and 5?

"He was one of the great financial journalists of our time," said Joseph Stiglitz, a professor at Columbia University in New York and the winner of a Nobel Prize for economics. "His death is shocking."

After that, the headlines kept breaking. The *New York Times*, the *Washington Post*, the *Financial Times*, MSNBC, NPR...

Mark always felt sure he would win the lawsuit, especially when the appeal went all the way to the Supreme Court. We talked about it a lot: the case, the crash, who was involved, exactly how America was headed for a huge financial fall. It was riveting. And frightening, especially when he explained how it would directly affect the economy and people's lives.

Later that year, Congress would authorize $700 billion for a bank bailout in what became one of the most universally hated things Congress has ever done. At the same time, the Fed had a bailout going that was potentially in the multiple trillions of dollars.

But before the appeals court ruled in Mark's favor, he was already... you-know-what.

The timing of his death made for much bigger news in some circles than it might have otherwise. Some people actually *believed* he could have been *murdered,* by the government, for knowing more than he should have, for uncovering something they didn't want the public to know, or even as a warning to others, payback for exposing the truth.

His writing partner wanted to tell me this part in person. He took a car service from the city to bring us lunch: two Katz's deli sandwiches, pastrami on rye.

"Why would anyone think Mark was murdered?" I asked putting the sandwich down on a plate, still not fully understanding how the information had the power to implode the global economy.

While we laughed off the ridiculousness of it all, Bob and I agreed it was nevertheless important to alert the medical examiner. You know, just in case.

I handed him the phone. "Yes, any kind of foul play whatsoever. And screenings for poison," I heard him say as he walked back and forth between the dining and the living room, conferring with the medical examiner about the rumors. "Yes, I'm sitting with the widow now," Bob confirmed.

It was the first time I heard someone call me a widow, and even with everything else happening in that moment, it's that first reference that I remember most vividly.

Widow.

I've come to hate the word more than any other, even more than "no." And I have *always* hated the word "no."

12

Knock-Knock, Please Don't Be There

"You stand yourself up against the winds of
familiar voices and the flash of their faces,
grasping for steadiness against humanity."

—Excerpted from Mark's journals

As word spread, friends and neighbors converged on our house like an accident scene you just can't turn away from.

Meanwhile I was still trapped inside the mangled car but was almost expected to stay in the wreckage while people watched me hanging there, upside down, chunks of glass matted in my stiff, bloody hair.

At first, I tried to ward visitors off by putting a note on the door: WE'RE NAPPING. Some still knocked; a few walked in anyway. One came right into my bedroom—at 6:30 am—to say she knew she would find me there, finally sleeping.

Then there was the phone. It kept *ringing*. When I turned the cell phone off, the house phone would ring. When I unplugged the house phone, the cell phone went off. Sometimes they both rang at the same time.

What is it about a ringing phone that compels you to pick it up?

We all know how it feels to be told to sit down. What follows is usually devastating news.

We rush into action; we want to help, to let the family know how much we care. We pick up the phone; we send a text or an email; we send flowers and food and sympathy cards. We show up at the house, shocked and devastated, hoping to connect with the family and other friends, to share the sadness.

I know why they thought it would help to share their stories with me, so the girls and I didn't feel so alone in our grief. But it just upset me more to hear about other people losing their babies, spouses, mothers, fathers, sisters, brothers, best friends, ex-husbands, lovers, sisters-in-law, cats—anyone and everyone, it seemed. It also made me feel guilty and horrible that Mark's death had brought it all back up for them.

Ring, ring.

"Hello?" Damn it. Why did I pick up again?

And why, of all people, did it have to be Pia?

She was one of those people who never remembered meeting you despite being introduced countless times.

Who knows; maybe she saw me as one of her charity cases? A volunteer opportunity? A Junior League flunky?

"Yes, of course I know who you are, Pia." (*You snubbed me at the Gerber's barbecue just last week and now feel impossibly guilty about it*). "Mmm-hmm...yes...uh-huh...Thank you, we'd love to have your casserole." (*But actually, no thank you. Truth is, I don't want to eat your casserole. I never wanted to eat your casserole. And now I never will eat your casserole just because my husband is dead. Calm down, Laura. Breathe...what'd she say? Well, it was less than seventy-two hours ago so, no, Pia, this is not a good time to call...*)

Inside voices. Play the part, Laura; be nice, even though Pia's prattling on and on like pink cotton candy.

"Mmm-hmm...oh, that would be lovely, thank you, Pia. Why, yes, you certainly did accomplish a lot today, with the garden fundraiser and dropping Indiana at his acrobatic fencing class before picking up Luna from her gluten-free cooking lessons." (*One wonders to think how you possibly had time to bake a casserole for poor, widow me.*) "How nice...yes, it sounds like you *will* have time to shower and get ready to meet your husband for dinner in the city by 6:30, provided you pick up the nanny early and then get to my house to drop off the *casserole* in between." (*Thank you so much for reminding me that I will never have dinner with my husband ever again.*) "Sure, anytime is great." (*I'll be home crying for the next few years, so my schedule will be quite flexible.*)

What else was I supposed to do? Wrap my hands around my throat and squeeze as hard as I could until my eyeballs popped out like meatballs?

13

Blast from the Past

"Samuel swung open the leather hinged door
and stomped the snow from his boots. His
daughters slept on the floor beneath a huge
pile of skins. He built a fire in the hearth
and was soon satisfied with the fire's life."

—Excerpted from Mark's journals

It was now almost a week later—the night before the funeral. People had begun filing into the house because that's what you do, right? You show up. You hug, you cry, and you eat Pia's casserole.

The only person missing was my father, Robert.

It had been more than forty years since he walked out on us to marry his executive secretary and take on her brood of six children from a previous marriage.

Back then, we were the only fatherless family in town. I can remember deciding at age six that I would never marry anyone or have children. That way, I reasoned, no one would ever leave us and make us cry. That stood in direct contrast to TV commercial fantasy and fairy tale storybooks spoon-feeding little girls tales of happily ever after, the ones Barbie doll dreams are made of.

Growing up, my father never tried to be a parent. We only saw him about a dozen times throughout the years, and while I always hoped for some sort of apology or explanation, all we ever got were disappearing acts.

Yet here was Mark, proudly wearing the fatherhood badge of honor, making special plans with Maggie, his daughter from his first marriage. He saw her during the week and on weekends, never missing whatever was important to her. Once, he drove almost three hours just to meet her for lunch at a ski lodge in the Catskills during a junior high school trip.

I sometimes told her just how lucky she was to have a father at all, much less one who would do that, as if any eleven-year-old would understand.

More importantly, it was by watching their father-daughter relationship that I became hopeful, even confident, that when our own children came, I wouldn't worry for them. Or for me. While Robert was now on his third wife and possibly counting, Mark and I had been totally solid.

I sat in the living room that night, studying my mom's face, as people filed into the house to pay their respects. I remembered her grief when my father left and how she had teared up behind her fashionably big sunglasses and Jackie-O scarves whenever Dionne Warwick came on the eight-track player in our brown Chevy Suburban, singing "One Less Bell to Answer." I now understood why she played that song over and over again; it's for the same reasons I played "American Pie" over and over again, ever since the doctor told me to prepare to become Mark's widowed bride.

A knock on the door snapped me back. Amazingly, there stood my father, Robert, with a bouquet of flowers in hand. I found myself collapsing into his arms, heaving tears as he held me for the first time since I was a little girl. He apologized for leaving and explained that accumulated guilt had stood in the way of him being a father.

The longer he waited, the worse it got, he said. Then he avoided it altogether.

He patiently answered all my questions, steadying himself against the house as I clung to him. He stroked my hair, kissed my forehead, and wiped the sleeve of his beautiful dress shirt across my drooling nose.

"You can do this, Laura," was the last thing he said before leading me back into the house where he added more logs to the fire.

14

F is for Funeral

"God demands a sacrifice from each of us as we resist the ultimate sacrifice we must make in order to obtain eternal life. I bowed my head in silent prayer and the rest did the same. It was a day of grief."

—Excerpted from Mark's journals

It's hard to say which was worse—watching the girls hold hands to walk down the church aisle, seeing the anguished looks on the faces of Mark's family, or having the Reverend unexpectedly hand me the box of ashes just as it was my turn to go.

It was my first time seeing Mark since leaving him at the hospital. And now, here he was: in a black box, which I was expected to carry like a baby to the front of the church before placing him on a display table. The whole thing seemed a little heavy-handed and, frankly, quite morbid. But it was too late; the awful organ music had already started.

Forward, march.

Don't make eye contact, I told myself, or you won't be able to stop crying. Just walk. You can do it, Laura.

I made it to the end of the impossibly long aisle, barely, but how was I supposed to leave him alone up there? Just place him down on the designated table and take a seat? Really? I did what I was told, though in my mind we sat together that day.

"I'm glad you chose the black box instead of the gray or blue one," I leaned over to tell him. "It looks great on you."

Then he would smile and whisper something naughty in my ear about what my hot black funeral dress was doing to him and how he couldn't wait to get me home and take it off. I'd smile back, squeezing his hand, grateful to have his love at a terrible time like this.

Pretending to have him there next to us, even if it was in a box, meant that we were a whole family again, attending the funeral of someone else's poor dead husband.

Yes, it's a terrible tragedy, I know. Oh, this is our daughter, Nell. Nice to meet you. Nell is in fifth grade. Our other daughter is Susannah; say hello, Susannah. She's eight and yes, she does look older. She's tall, just like her father. Oh yes, and this is my tall husband, Mark. He's 6'4", but you can't really tell because he's dead and they burned his body and packed him into the box that's sitting here with us instead of on stage because I don't want people's last memory of him to be in a box. I'm his wife, Laura, keeper of the box. It's just awful. Such a good guy. His family must be devastated. Yes, you take care, too.

It really was a good thing I didn't hold the service at the little church next door, where everyone would hold hands and walk back up the hill to our house afterwards for a light lunch. The church needed to hold hundreds of people—827, to be exact—not counting the TV crew or the police directing traffic and managing the chartered busloads of Bloomberg people who were driven in from the city.

My Aunt Sally, a Lutheran minister, flew in to give the service alongside the reverend of the church. Even though Mark was a Christian, Bob Dylan was his true religion. I asked that they replace some of the moaning, groaning organ music with "Blowin' in the Wind."

How many roads must a man walk down
Before you call him a man?
How many seas must a white dove sail
Before she sleeps in the sand?
Yes, how many times must the cannonballs fly
Before they're forever banned?
The answer, my friend, is blowin' in the wind
The answer is blowin' in the wind.

The eulogies were really good, whatever that means. Billy had a cold, but still braved the microphone to say some really nice things that made everyone feel a little bit better.

I don't really remember much from mine, other than people laughing when I explained our goal in life: to raise our daughters to be able to dine with the queen and pee in the woods.

No one seemed surprised that Mark had returned an unused $800 auto parts reimbursement check to GEICO, either. That's my husband; always the Boy Scout. But Mark always tried to do the right thing, which taught my bad Girl Scout self the value of good karma (and to iron her uniform daily).

Bob gave a eulogy that was both hard-hitting and full of praise for Mark's work, his strong love of family, and his taste for Jack Daniels. But when he addressed the murder conspiracy—right there, front and center in the middle of the service—I felt a tingle of paranoia wash over me.

The culprit often stands behind the crime tape watching the action, right? Well, they also often attend the dead guy's funeral in an effort to look innocent.

Knowing this, I began scanning faces, looking for clues. Perhaps it was that man—the one standing alone in the back of the church in the pink tie. Who was he, anyway? Or maybe there was more than one assassin? Maybe it was that group of people standing over there? They looked government-like, for sure. Guilty, even.

After about an hour, it was time to go; the reverend's hand was on my shoulder, steering me and the girls back down the aisle.

Mark's company graciously hosted a beautiful food and wine-fueled reception at Alder Manor in Yonkers, a partially abandoned castle Mark and I had discovered on a hilly walk one day. It had become one of our favorite places to explore, with all its secret rooms and libraries full of cracked leather-bound books.

Karma Girl Scout had a little slip-up, albeit an understandable one, in taking a memento from a large library in the castle—a copy of *War and Peace*. To me, the title summarized Mark's life of war with the Federal Reserve and his finding peace in heaven. When it made its way into my bag, I figured it was the book's fault for being in the wrong place at the right time.

The party, if you want to call it that, proved to be what everyone needed—a big, beautiful celebration of Mark's big, beautiful life. At one point, I found myself trapped in the ladies' room with a well-meaning friend when I heard Mark's booming voice.

There he was on a big projector screen talking and laughing; the filmmakers of *American Casino* had put together an outtake reel of Mark from the movie.

I quickly found my way to the kitchen, where no one would see me crying except the poor, kind Latino caterers.

"Lady, you okay?" asked one. "You are sad. Very sad. For you, I am sorry," he apologized, and handed me a plum.

15

The Shot Heard
Round the World

"The reality is that there is no reality. It's
all a fabrication of unknowns in seeking
truths."

—Excerpted from Mark's journals

When everything died down (pardon the pun), I found myself finally alone for the first time in more than nine days. Well, almost alone; my mother and stepfather were staying on for a few weeks to help, but right now they were upstairs with the girls.

It was the perfect time to hit the Internet. A quick Google search for "Mark Pittman" produced about 86,000 results in 0.42 seconds. Most of the hits continued reporting the news of his death, but more than a few focused on the alleged murder.

Maybe that's why I found a few people going through his desk drawers in the basement after the funeral reception while everyone else was upstairs sipping coffee and eating baked goods? Maybe they were looking for something really B-I-G.

Part of me somehow wanted the conspiracy theories to be true—to explain my senseless loss, to give me something to rail against. The other part of me obviously didn't.

The theories leaned toward the provocative, as conspiracy theories tend to do. Some were wackier than others; stories of government agents in dark coats using an umbrella to fire a toxin-tipped dart (ingredients presumed to be one gram. of shellfish toxin and eight milligrams of cobra venom) into some guy's heart.

The other one was a more garden-variety method of poisoning, which had Mark dying from lethal food poisoning. Maybe the big bad government officials paid off the Turkish food cart guy on 47th and Lex to poison Mark's morning egg white and turkey bacon bagel sandwich?

Fiction is better than fact, and much more entertaining, which makes it almost inevitable to see this sort of mass-appeal fodder erupt amongst the wing nuts when a high-profile person drops dead.

That's not to say that everyone whispering "conspiracy" was wearing tinfoil hats. Some people began telling me they believed it. "I *have* to talk to you about Mark," they would say, followed by, "I think he was poisoned," or "Don't you think the timing is suspicious?" "Who vomits blood during a heart attack?" What's more, "Who vomits blood and has a heart attack in the middle of a lawsuit against the government?"

Then they would reference people like Vince Foster, a Deputy White House Counsel during Clinton's administration who "committed suicide" over the Travelgate scandal by "shooting himself" in the head. Or Karen Silkwood, who "crashed her car" the night before blowing the whistle on her plutonium-loving bosses. Later, they would bring up Andrew Breitbart, a reporter who also "dropped dead of a heart attack" the day before releasing information thought to be critically damaging to Barack Obama prior to the election. (People still really like that one, given the basic facts of

Mark's death. Here were two prominent journalists on the verge of releasing major stories that threatened the government, both who miraculously dropped dead of "heart attacks" before going to press.)

Even my own very level-headed parents were becoming paranoid, especially after seeing "suspicious" cars parked across the street. They reported how the drivers would sit there for a few hours at a time without ever getting out. Sometimes it would be a different man, which suggested they were working in shifts.

Who knows who they were or why they were there, I said, but it wasn't like they were going come and shoot us between the eyes. They were probably just livery drivers waiting for their passengers. Or, maybe they were reporters doing the same thing Mark and I had done: park outside the home waiting for a lucky break. It didn't occur to me until later to think, "If those were reporters outside the house, why didn't they just come and knock on the door?" But by then, it was too late; they were gone.

"Pay attention."

That was all the voice on the other end of the phone said before hanging up, leaving me stunned and shaking.

"What's wrong, Mom?" the girls asked. "Are you having a heart attack, too?"

"No, sillies, I'm just really cold," I told them. "Will you both go upstairs and grab me a sweater each? See if you can find a pink one and a green one." I didn't own a sweater of either color; that was the point.

Another call came from a woman who read about Mark in the newspaper and warned me not speak to anyone about his death "in order to safeguard my beautiful family."

"Oh, thank you very much," I replied, acting as normal as possible as the girls sat at the table, happily eating their peanut butter and jelly sandwiches. "I'll be sure to make note of that."

"Who was that, Mom?" Nell asked.

"Oh, some lady selling Avon."

That call was obviously from a looney. But there *was* one that really got me going. The well-spoken man identified himself as an attorney in Washington, D.C. He didn't sound insane at all; but that's probably proof that he was. He told me to listen carefully, that Mark had been poisoned and that I needed to be careful of what I said and who I talked to, including the medical examiner. Then he hung up. Caller ID didn't ID; it was an unknown caller.

"Laura? Laura!" my mother started calling from the basement. "You have to get rid of this."

"Get rid of what?" I asked snottily, as I headed downstairs. It drives me crazy when someone calls out to me from other rooms in the house. Growing up, it was usually to help find her hairbrush, something my sister and I still joke about today.

She was poking at a box of poison mouse pellets as if it would jump out and eat her alive. "The poison that's right there," she said. "You don't want to get blamed."

"Jesus Christ, Mom!" I exclaimed. "No one is going to blame me!"

"Is that language necessary?" My mother does *not* appreciate swearing or the taking of the Lord's name in vain. But what does she expect, when no one bothered to have me baptized? Besides, everyone says Jesus Christ, even in church, *especially* in church.

16

The Five W's: Who, What, Where, Why, When (and How)

"Bad pounding dream waking now. Sheets covered
in her scent. Her chest heaving as she
breathes to steady consciousness."

—Excerpted from Mark's journals

I sometimes lay in bed, thinking about who would want to murder Mark, what they murdered him with, where they did it, why they did it, when they did it, and how they did it. All good, solid questions.

In the "good" dreams, Mark would do things like drive off into the sky in a convertible, waving and smiling at me. Happy to be off on an adventure, he would nonetheless look wistful while telling me how he "had to go now." Or I'd see him sitting on the sidelines, smiling as he watched the girls from afar. But when I reached out to him, he turned into black and white TV static dots and vanished, leaving me frantically searching the playground for him until desperate panic woke me up.

And the bad dreams? Those were *bad.*

"It's 997 Broadway!" I would shout into the phone as Mark thrashed on the floor in front of me. But the 911 operator just kept saying how she couldn't hear me and to "repeat the location."

In the really bad ones, I could hear him screaming for me to get help, but every door I ran to was locked. I watched as men fed him poison while dangling a mouse in his face.

Another would see me racing home from the restaurant to find him shot dead, surgical instruments protruding from his heart.

In all the dreams, he was wearing a red shirt.

I began to dread going to sleep and would wrap his box of ashes in a towel and strap it to my chest with one of his belts to help keep my heart from beating too fast, like one of those dog thunder vests. But it didn't work; the plastic box was too hard and uncomfortable. And it didn't stop the dreams.

My family, Amy, even my closest friends all said the same thing: that this was all a normal reaction to stress and that I would be "fine."

But what if the dreams were somehow true? Then what? If it *was* murder, someone had to have done it; the guy didn't pour himself a cup of coffee and add arsenic to it or prick himself with a poison heart dart.

And if the government did it, wouldn't they have already had me framed, or at least tried in the court of public opinion courtesy of a manic media attack? After all, who's the most likely suspect in these cases? Me! The spouse! Anyone who watches TV knows that the first suspects are usually family members, the ones who cry and plead for the public to come forward with information about their loved one.

I laid there, imagining the autopsy report being delivered in a squad car, followed by a SWAT team storming my house and ripping me away from my children. Nell and Susannah would be left standing on the porch, screaming, "Don't take my Mommy!" as dozens of tipped-off reporters creep through the yard or park their giant satellite dishes out front, shoving TV cameras in my face.

"Mrs. Pittman! Did you kill your husband?"

"Tell us in your own words, why did you poison your husband?"

"In Yonkers, New York, this is Katy Chang reporting live from outside the house of the accused Pittman poisoner."

17

Just the Facts, Ma'am

"I was slipping and I knew it. My
convalescence was difficult, as chest wounds
take months to heal. I was just getting my
strength back when specks of blood started to
fill my handkerchief and the cramps started."

—Excerpted from Mark's journals

You never really think about how important each moment of life is until you're forced to examine every second of it.

I needed to know: could I have somehow saved him? Or was he truly dead the second he hit the ground? The only way to find out was to get a copy of the ambulance report. So what if I begged the desk manager to break the rules. I needed a copy of the report and I needed it now.

Narrative: 23:16:00. 52 yo male in cardiac arrest on the second-floor hallway. CPR started by YPD at the scene. IV est in rt ac with 18 gage cath and saline lock. Pt asystole on monitor and fire advised me that their AED said no shock advised. Administered epi and atropine as per protocol; no change. Pt had the start of rigor in jaw and hard to open mouth, so inserted a king airway without problem. Capnography good, epi and atropine administered without change. 23:34. Txp to closest facility, ed notified of patient condition.

You know how they say people can survive for up to six minutes without oxygen before permanent brain damage kicks in? This meant the ambulance would need to have reached him by 23:10:00, as opposed to 23:16:00.

I've also heard that the body and brain can survive longer at lower temperatures, like in frozen ponds. So why couldn't he have fallen into the bathtub, and somehow hit the cold water knob on the way down?

Or what about the scenario in which everything went perfectly— the one where he was brought back to life through CPR, IVs, intubation, or AED paddles?

But the question remained. Would he have had any quality of life or would he have been reduced to sitting in front of a blaring TV all day?

Not so fast, Fahrenthold, says the American Heart Association. You'd really need a miracle, babe; fewer than eight percent of the 383,000 people who suffer cardiac arrest outside of a hospital each year survive.

I'm sorry for all of them and for anyone who goes through this, but the only person I really care about here is Mark. What about *him*?

And really, what about *me*? Did I do anything wrong? Did I act quickly enough? Did I do it hard enough? Too hard? The questions tortured me.

There was no way to be sure without expert interpretation. I took the report *back* to the source: the ambulance station. Only my guy wasn't at the desk.

What does this mean and what does that mean?

Verification, please.

"What? You can't talk to me about my own husband? Why not? Fine, here's my ID. I am his wife. And if you want to get right down to it, I am your customer. I hired you to do a job, I am the one who will be paying the bill, and now I need to review the job so I can understand the service you provided."

You'll need to write to my supervisor.

"Are you freaking kidding me? I don't have time to write to your supervisor. I need answers *now*."

I'm sorry, ma'am.

"Really? You're sorry? Well, just so you know, I will *never* call 911 again!"

An EMT friend offered to give an unofficial assessment of the report. A few minutes in, she shook her head and told me there was nothing I could have done.

My own physician concurred after reading it, too, explaining that CPR in and of itself does not save anyone's life, that it is designed to "buy time." But in Mark's case, he said, there simply *was* no time. He was gone the second he hit the ground and there was no amount of CPR that I or anyone else could have done to save him.

18

The Red Envelope, Please

"The only coincidences are the ones God creates to give answers and meaning to those needing it most."

—Excerpted from Mark's journals

My only escape from life came in the form of little red envelopes. Movies from Netflix, shipped straight to my door.

"*The Diving Bell and the Butterfly* is here, Mom," the girls called excitedly, rushing up the stairs holding the envelope like a goldfish they had won at the fair.

I had never heard of the movie, and knew the girls hadn't ordered it, either.

Oh great, I thought. *Better not tell my stepfather I couldn't even keep a Netflix account straight.* Before he and my mother left to return home, George had carefully laid out an entire five page to-do list for me: call the bank and the insurance company; sign and mail these documents with death certificates attached; write these checks; mail these bills; call Nationwide—you need these papers to get the title to your car; send this letter certified mail.

Who cares if Netflix was messed up, on top of every other account that got messed up since I'd taken over the bills? *(Correction: Since the outdoor grill had taken over the bills. Burning everything proved much easier than spending my life sorting through fifteen years of paperwork to find receipts. The bill collectors knew where to find me; we could start over from there.)*

I called Netflix. They checked; their records showed I had ordered the movie.

"There must be a mistake," I told the man on the phone. "I've never heard of it, and certainly did not order it. We're waiting for *Alvin and the Chipmunks*, not this...diving bell movie."

He issued a credit, adding that I could go ahead and watch it while waiting for the right movie to arrive.

"No thanks," I said, putting it straight back into the mailbox.

But a week or so later, the same stupid movie showed up again. I called Netflix back, explaining that if I did not order it the first time, I definitely didn't order it a second time, and asked them to please stop sending it to me.

"Well, someone out there clearly wants you to watch it," a different customer service guy joked. "If I were you, I'd see what it's about. Free of charge."

So, one night I did.

The movie was based on a true story of a French *Vogue* magazine editor who suffered a massive stroke that left him with a condition known as locked-in syndrome, which meant that he was mentally aware but paralyzed from the neck down. Completely unable to speak. Just one functioning eye.

Undeterred, he developed a system of communication with his speech and language therapist by blinking his left eye as she called out letters. Using this tedious method, he laboriously spelled out his messages, letter by letter, eventually "dictating" an entire book about what it was like to be trapped in his own body. He likened the experience to being inside of an old-fashioned deep-sea diving suit, while those around him see his spirit, still alive, as a butterfly.

Soon after the book was published, he suffocated to death on his own mucous.

I will always wonder if Mark somehow sent me that movie to show me what could have happened had he survived and that living is not always a better alternative to dying.

19
Merry
First Christmas
Without You

"Samuel wandered into the woods, dragging an
ax through the snow-covered forest, his gaze
fixing upon an unsuspecting evergreen tree.
He felled it in three swift chops, much to
the amazement of his small children, who
delighted in the Christmas tradition."

—Excerpted from Mark's journals

Having never really liked the holidays to begin with, I now completely dreaded them.

The closer we got, the further I wanted to run away from everyone and everything. I couldn't bear the thought or the sight of all the happy, complete families who filled their houses with piano music and heartfelt toasts, where everyone erupted in laughter at the same old jokes as they sipped Aunt Terry's homemade eggnog while the kids ripped open truckloads of presents.

I had felt this way going back to when my brother, sister, mom, and I sat there, divorced and dysfunctional, buried under the expectation that all should be jolly and happy because it was suddenly Christmas. It's not that my mother (and later, my step-father) did anything wrong. It's just that the scar of my father leaving never healed.

To me, a holiday was just another day—one more round of pretending our lives were like everybody else's. Only then, I had to do it with a smile on my face, wearing an uncomfortable dress at a fractured family table while saying things like, "Please pass the ham."

I vowed never to torture my own children by pretending that "it's a wonderful life." Still, I fought my feelings by cleaning the house, washing my grandmother's china, setting out a few family photos, printing the same grocery list I had made the year before but never used. But all that did was remind me of my mother trying so hard for everyone to *be jolly and happy,* and then I would give up.

Even now, I still wear a certain brand of sadness, one that becomes more and more punctuated the closer we get to the "most magical time of year."

The girls and I received several invitations to spend that first Christmas with friends. Thanks, but no thanks; I could already see myself cast as the poor lonely widow with her dirty-faced children, ripping at the bread loaf and shoving candies in their pockets when no one was looking.

Didn't they have some homeless people to feed?

Distraction was the easiest way to cope and I was going to do it in style. Sold on words like "opulent" and "bohemian," I booked a hotel room to escape the holiday hatch.

The greatest thing about children is they'll happily go anywhere with you.

"Merry Christmas!" I cheered, waking them up. "Mommy has a big surprise for you: we're going to the city to stay at the W Hotel!"

"OK, Mommy," chirped my sleepy baby birds.

"Merry Christmas, Momma," Nell said sweetly, giving me kisses. "You're the best Mom in the whole world." And she meant it.

"I love you, Mom," Susannah added brightly, peeking up at me from under my white duvet, where the three of us had taken to sleeping together.

Thanks to free American Express points, the city would be a nice diversion, away from everyone and everything.

It wasn't until we went out for a nice dinner that I realized my mistake. We should have stayed home.

"A table for four please," I told the hostess, as cheerfully as I could. Nell immediately elbowed me.

"Ouch! Sorry. I mean a table for three, please." It wasn't worth explaining. The girls and I giggled about it, but once we entered the dining room, the laughter stopped. The three of us instead stood there clutching each other, crying.

We hadn't realized that entire families go out to dinner on Christmas. Here we were, looking to avoid the happiness of others, surrounded by tables *full* of festive family cheer.

It was pretty clear that this "Merry Christmas" thing just wasn't working out.

Christmas miracles typically hinge on a magical event, right?

In ours, I imagined Mark walking barefoot through the front door to find his shoes exactly where I had left them for him, like two plates of cookies for Santa. Then he would grab me and kiss me and twirl the girls in the air giving helicopter rides.

After that lovely homecoming scene, we would sit down to a traditional goose dinner. Later, after tucking the girls into bed, he would explain the whole story about how he got amnesia and had no identification on him when the police found him robbed, beaten up, and left for dead in an alley after getting off at the wrong train stop. It had taken thirty long days, but his memory came back and here he was. Home again!

We would talk and laugh into the night, and then he would carry me upstairs to our bedroom, where he would kiss me exactly how he always kissed me and smell exactly how he smelled and smile exactly the way that he always smiled and take me to places no other man could. That's how I would know it was really him.

And then we would spend another 5,679 nights together, and another and another until we were so old that our children, though they found us burdensome, still brought our beautiful grandchildren to visit us at the nursing home. Until finally, one of us would slip away quietly into the night, followed by the other very shortly after the way that old couples often do. Then people would console the girls and bring them meatball casseroles and say, "At least they had a long life."

20

Happy Birthday to Me, I Look 103!

"My birthday is tomorrow. Then again, it could just be the calendar. It doesn't really matter how long it's been since birth, some are just awakening now. But me, I've been here for so long now. I feel like laying down along the side of the highway and letting a semi run over my head."

—Excerpted from Mark's journals

Funny. Most people get cards on their birthdays. Me? I got Mark's autopsy report.

At this point, it had been thirty-six long days of waiting...and wondering. How *did* Mark die? I figured if he *had* been murdered, the police would have been contacted by now.

But to my thinking, you can never be too sure.

What if there were gray areas? Unexplainable findings? Things that made no sense, or things they overlooked? Maybe he had a high level of seafood extract in his blood, indicating poisoning, and the medical examiner just figured he ate lots and lots of fish?

Tearing through the paper, I checked the long list of body parts submitted for toxicology against the autopsy procedure manual I found online to make sure nothing had been overlooked.

Blood? Check.

Eye fluid? Check.

Urine? Check.

Bile? Check.

Gastric contents? Check.

Parts of liver and brain? Check.

But why did he vomit blood?

The report revealed gastroesophageal laceration syndrome. Translation: bleeding from tears in the mucosa at the junction of the stomach and esophagus, usually caused by severe retching, coughing, or vomiting. It didn't say *why* this happened, why someone would cough or vomit so hard that it tore their esophagus. It just said it happened. Could it have something to do with getting a regular flu shot and a swine flu shot on the same day? Or did it mean he was *you-know-what.*

As I flipped through the pages, there was a lot I didn't understand. But there was one word I did: "natural," as in natural death. Cause? Acute myocardial infarction. Translation: Big heart attack.

A partial list of "Anatomical Findings" included:

1. "The body is a well-developed, well-nourished, white male, 75 inches or 6'4", and appears 52 years." Correct. My husband was 52 and well-fed, *by candlelight.* But why did the medical examiner have to go and ruin it by reporting: "The stomach serosa is unremarkable, and the stomach has 80 ml or ⅓ cup of black fluid with small meat pieces," instead of saying his last supper was a beautiful steak dinner with his daughters?

2. "The 1460-gram (3.21 lb.) brain is symmetric, pale." Hmm...the average male brain is 1360 grams, or 2.99 lbs., which meant Mark had 100 extra grams floating around in his head. Does that mean people

with bigger brains are smarter than those with smaller brains? And what was the average weight of oversized brains to begin with?

3. "Heart, Cardiomegaly, 670 grams or 1.48 lbs. Moderately enlarged and has left ventricular hypertrophy and dilation of the right ventricle." Google said the average heart weighs 255–312 grams, or 0.56–0.69 pounds. How was it possible Mark's heart *doubled in size* and his doctor never noticed? Or did Mark know and just not tell me?

The list went on but didn't report: "Patient appeared dead, but suddenly sat straight up, jumped down off the table and reported that he was 'fine' before walking out the door."

That's the kind of bedtime story I wanted, where the stuffed bunny gets "turned into real."

21

New Year,
New Everything

"She always had some kind of cause going.
Immigrant rights; education; health care;
shelter for the homeless. We made the scene,
carried signs and collected signatures. I met
a lot of good political people."

—Excerpted from Mark's journals

The thing about mourning is you have to find time for it between all the regular day-to-day stuff that still needs doing.

This included my new job as a press secretary to an elected official. Chuck wasn't what you would call a "conventional" politician; he stood up for what he believed in, even sometimes against popular opinion. People either loved him or... not so much.

It was my responsibility to manage his council communications, which, in a city of close to 200,000 constituents, involved fence-mending. I would research and script his speeches, anticipate questions and rehearse answers, or wildly gesture for him to *stop talking* when he had given a perfect sound bite, yet there were still times when his foot found its way into his mouth.

Still, I was firmly in the Pro-Chuck camp. He was hard-working, always listened to both sides, and stood up for his constituents. Still, I hated the job itself because of a senior level supervisor, whom we'll call Ms. Miserable, and her lackeys. She made every day a rained-out puppy parade in addition to being just plain old mean.

"I've had it Chuck. Didn't we all talk about this? Then you go say and do whatever you please? Why? Why do I bother?" she would rant.

SLAM! Went! Her! Office! Door!

I was a frequent target as well; Ms. M hated me more than cooked spinach.

In fairness, it wasn't really her fault. Some days she would give me detailed instructions to write a press release on something like the school budget or a new environmental impact study, and then every bit of detail would completely bypass my brain cells.

Amy, my stalwart therapist, explained that memory loss is one way your body copes with major stress. "It's totally normal to have staggering blanks as a result of trauma," she said in trying to reassure me. She even had a name for it: post-traumatic stress disorder.

"Don't you think that's a bit much?" I objected. "That's like my mother saying she has influenza instead of a common cold, or a compound fracture instead of just a broken toe."

According to Amy, it wasn't. Cortisol—the hormone responsible for stress—affects the glucocorticoid receptors in the hippocampus and prefrontal cortex, which directly impairs short-term memory, concentration and learning.

"How much of that cortisol stuff do you think is in there? Is it a tablespoon, or a gallon, or what?" I asked. "And can they drain it out if there's too much? Because honestly, the idea of having brain surgery sounds pretty appealing right about now."

At least she laughed.

"But seriously. Do you think I have it? What's it called again?"

Normally she would turn any questions back at me and make me talk about them for the forty-five-minute session.

Only this time, she didn't do that. She answered for me.

"Yes, I most definitely think you have it," she reported. "It's a classic case. No doubt at all. One hundred percent."

"Is there a cure?"

The answer was no.

"The prefrontal cortex plans complex cognitive behavior, personality expression, and decision-making, as well as moderates social behavior," she read from her purple notebook, looking up to make sure I was paying attention.

I wasn't, as it happened. I was playing cat's cradle with a rubber band.

She looked at me as if to say, "Please stop doing that."

How did she expect me to pay attention while sitting there telling me how I had difficulty paying attention?

It was much more interesting to create string figures and to wonder why my folder was purple. Did she have color coded files for each type of patient, like purple for the grievers as in purple hearts? Yellow for couples in counseling, until she could file them in folders of green for divorce or red for "stop, try again?" Gray would be the obvious color for the lonely and depressed, with blue for those who were not *clinically* depressed, just sad.

Put the rubber band down and pay attention, I told myself.

"It relates to the ability to differentiate among conflicting thoughts," I heard her continue, "it" referring to my cortisol-infused prefrontal cortex.

I hadn't heard a word she said. Instead I sat worrying. *What if my brain truly had shrunk, or was shrinking while we spoke? Could it regrow itself like an earthworm that gets chopped in two by a garden shovel? Or was it too late?*

That can happen you know. It *can* be too late.

"What number comes after 456?" she asked suddenly.

"457," I answered proudly.

"How are the girls?"

"Fine. They're good. They're adjusting pretty well, I think."

"What did you have for dinner last night?"

"Come on," I protested, "that's not fair. No one remembers what they had for dinner last night. Do *you* remember what *you* had for dinner last night?"

"Pasta primavera," she said flatly, as if the pronouncement somehow proved her point.

She changed subjects. "How is your mood?"

"I'm still crying a lot."

"Remember these five things," she said counting them out on her fingers. "Dog. Blue velvet. Volvo. Pen. Wire hanger."

"Wait," I pleaded. "You're going too fast."

"Do you think you could be depressed?"

"Sure, I'm depressed, but not *depressed,* depressed. At least, I don't think so. Maybe I'm too depressed to know if I am depressed."

"I don't see you as being depressed. Profoundly sad? Yes. Traumatized? Yes. But depressed, no."

"Okay, good. Me neither."

"How's work going?"

"I can't concentrate. I'm driving Ms. M crazy. I actually feel sorry for her; all she needs is for at least one of us to function like a normal human being, and I can't even do that.

"The other day, I was on deadline and she found me in the empty courtroom instead. I go in there when I know I'm going to cry. Sometimes it's only once or twice a day, but I've never been able to make it a whole day. It's a lot like peeing, you know? No one goes a full day without peeing, especially if your body's full of water or tears and cortisol or whatever you called it; I have to go a lot."

"Have you considered family leave?"

I had, but who can afford to take 12 weeks off without pay?

"You get four days paid bereavement leave on national average, and that's *it*," I reported. "Crazy, right? Your house could blow up and all your kids could get killed, but you have to put on a suit and show up at work as if nothing happened four days later."

"Did you make your bed today?"

"I never make my bed. It's a duvet; you just pull up, no tuck and fold."

"OK, now give me the list. Do you remember the five things?"

"Umm..." I thought for a moment. "Blue velvet. Volvo. Cat. Pen... cil? House. Clothes hangers? I forgot the last one. Did you say roses?"

"First, there were only five items, not seven. It was dog, blue velvet, Volvo, pen, wire hanger."

"Oh."

She handed me a list of brain exercises. She expected me to fill in index cards with important dates and events in history, do crossword puzzles, track a rolling marble in a cake pan, all in hopes of sparking some brain waves into action.

She also softly and kindly suggested joining a parent-to-parent/ peer bereavement group. I had never been one to join a group, ever, much less a pathetic griever's group. But okay, let me try it. Who knows? It might help the girls.

22

AA for Dead People

"Insanity is rife these days lately. The reality of the situation is so intense that something inside nearly everyone snaps and what you have left is simply a quivering mass of humanity. One minute involved in some sort of grandiose fantasy, the next unable to control a frenzy of grief."

—Excerpted from Mark's journals

I'm fine," I told the lady organizing the bereavement group. "I'm really only here to help my kids."

Her eyes said "Really?" but her trained voice told me that it was okay, that I could take my time.

I called it AA for Dead People. Granted, I've never been to an AA meeting, but it was easier to make jokes than admit to being part of a bereavement group. Wasn't that sort of thing for men with baggy plaid pants pulled up to their armpits and old ladies with blue hair?

The meetings started with introductions: name, who had died, when, and how.

"Hi, I'm Marco."

"Hi, Marco," the room echoed in unison.

"My wife Fabiana died on October 17. She had a stroke."

The structured words rang out like microphone checks, testing us to see if we could at least hear what we could not yet accept. Sitting there on those hard, wooden chairs in a private Bronxville, NY school classroom, week after week, listening to people's stories... this was really painful stuff: a drowned alcoholic husband whose body didn't surface for a week; a teenage daughter's suicide; a father of four who got pinned under his car. There was even a guilty admission of infidelity. Listening was like being given the choice between freezing to death or burning to death—no right answer.

Our children were sequestered downstairs in their own groups, talking about their feelings while painting pictures, playing games, decorating cakes, and making "memory pillows."

My girls went on a scavenger hunt at home, collecting everything from pocket knives and baby pictures to his socks and even a box of goldfish food to stuff in their pillows.

They didn't talk about what they did in their groups, and I was careful not to intrude. When they did ask me something, I answered them honestly and directly. I also made sure to include them in all decisions, big and small; from, "Do you want to go to the funeral home with me to pick up extra urns for the family?" to "Do you want cookies for dinner and pizza for breakfast, or pizza for dinner and cookies for breakfast?"

Being in the group helped me realize two things: first, that my kids were amazingly resilient, and second, that the bereaved do weird things, like leave the front door unlocked in hopes their lost loved one will come home or pour them morning cups of coffee. I suppose that explains my wearing his jockey shorts under my funeral dress to give me super strength to get through the day. Sometimes, I still sleep in them, but don't tell anybody.

Of course, none of these actions changed reality...he wasn't walking through the front door to have coffee with me in his underwear.

I told the group not to feel any worse for me than the next person; in fact, I was incredibly grateful for having been there with him; to be able to comfort him and tell him how much he was loved.

Mark knew if he had died without me, I would have gone crazy with the questioning. OK, *crazier with the questioning.* I'm convinced that's why he floated me up with him in his final moments. He wanted me to know, to really understand, that his life was not over, that people really do have spirits that live beyond the vessels that house them.

I never believed that to be true, or even possible. That was a platitude for hippy dippy New Agers or the super religious, I thought. But I now had proof. And knowing his spirit or energy or atoms or whatever are buzzing around *somewhere* in the world is extraordinary.

I tried explaining the out-of-body experience and the blown-out window to my closest friends and family, but it seemed to make them pity me, as if I had imagined the events to ease my trauma. Well, maybe all but his friend Mike, who came to fix the window the next day, seeing it with his own eyes. But at grief group, no one questioned it. Some had similar experiences of witnessing what we called the "lift off," though my experience was definitely more profound since Mark was not resigned to dying in a hospital bed.

23

All the Livelong Day

"Need some space, time. Stop running, moving, sit still. Take on new horizons. Retrace karma by chanting mantras."

—Excerpted from Mark's journals

Office politics continued in stark contrast to the hug-it-out sessions at bereavement group. At least we were heading into summer; everyone knows that's when government is even more slow-acting and when it's quiet enough to hear an earring drop.

Literally.

"What was that noise?" Ms. M asked, looking up from my newsletter copy. She loved editing my copy—to death, usually. Sometimes she would make me wait for days; other times, she pounced. Today had been a pouncing day.

She was in full form, decked out in all her glory. She acted as though the sound of the dropped earring was an elephant storming the hallways, causing the marble halls to crack and the chandeliers to fall crashing to the floor.

I could see the silver post on the floor by her left foot. Bad; I would have to ask her to move, something I dreaded. Worse, I would need to bend down to pick it up. Worst of all, I might have to get on my hands and knees to do it.

"Um..." I spoke up. "My earring; it's under your foot. Would you mind moving, so I can grab it?"

No response. Maybe she hadn't heard me. I tried again, a little louder. This time she stepped aside.

"Thank you," I said.

"You're welcome," she replied.

But we both knew she didn't mean it.

I needed air. Maybe this was what they called the ANGER STAGE—where a person sees more red than any other color in the rainbow, or when they do things despite themselves.

The Hudson View Deli was the place to go if you needed cat litter, a dozen eggs, or were craving a Twinkie. It was also perfect for candy, newspapers and...well, cigarettes.

Yes, I know I shouldn't have been smoking.

"Tough day at the office?" asked the man behind the counter, eyeing me curiously as he turned over a pack of American Spirits. Or should I say, sizing me up curiously; he wasn't looking me up and down or anything suggestive. He just stared straight into my eyes, almost holding me in place. It felt a little uncomfortable.

"What makes you say that?" I asked, looking away quickly.

"Just a feeling I get," he replied.

More silence. More staring.

"It's like..." he started, struggling to put it in words. "It's like you're here, but you're really not."

"Well, I'd rather not be here at all, but I am," I muttered. "In Yonkers, I mean. Not in life."

"Sounds like someone needs a vacation."

"Oh, yeah. Wouldn't that be nice? To just take off? Leave your life behind?"

"You should think about it." He suddenly sounded serious. "Everyone can use a break. Go someplace nice."

And that was that. I didn't think much of the exchange, really, until a few weeks later when something besides the cigarettes drew me back.

"So, did you think about it? What we talked about?" he asked, leaning against the counter.

We hadn't gone anywhere since the girls were little. Between Mark's job and my worry that he would somehow die from the airplane pressure and end up being flown home in a body bag, it wasn't really a priority.

"A change of scenery is good for people, you know," he told me. "It can make you remember who you are and help decide a new direction in life."

"What are you, some kind of mind reader?" He sure didn't look like a mind reader; don't mind readers wear turbans and smell like sandalwood incense? This guy was wearing a checkered shirt, pens lined neatly in the pocket, with his hair heavily matted down with gooey gel.

"Why, yes, I am. Or so people tell me," he declared, beaming with obvious pride. "And you, I can read."

Who was this mysterious guru who could pick up on things that I wasn't sure I wanted to reveal, especially by a stranger? That's one sure way to keep me smoke-free, I thought.

But of course, I went sailing back all too soon.

"Hey, Deli Man," I called out as I walked in, trying to keep the mood light. "Got smokes?"

I'm not sure if he thought it was funny, but I did.

"You again?" He handed me a single cigarette and a book of matches. "Here. They're called loosies; that way, you can buy one or two instead of a whole pack."

Was it legal? No, but it helped keep my lungs Girl Scout pink.

"Why are you still here?"

"Why am I still here?" I asked. "I'll tell you why, Deli Man. I am still here because I *have* to still be here. You know, a job and kids, house, car, bills? Stuff like that. Otherwise, believe me—I'd be outta here faster than you could say 'summer vacation.'"

A big smile landed on his face.

"Forget all of that," he insisted. "It's almost the first official day of summer. You need some time and space to sit still. Chant some mantras."

"What does that mean, chant mantras? You mean like in yoga or meditation or whatever when you repeat a phrase over and over again until you pass out from the reverberating bliss of it all?"

"You'll see," he continued smiling.

No I won't, I thought, as I walked out carrying the bag of Foster's beer and a whole pack of cigarettes. I'll be fine.

Part II:
The First Trip:
What I Did on My
Summer Vacation

24

Breaking Good

"I jump started my hog and pointed it away far from my life. Sometimes gas makes you forget quicker than booze when all you see are the miles of road ahead."

—Excerpted from Mark's journals

At least, I *thought* I'd be fine. But it's hard to make progress, to "move through the stages," when there's always something there to remind you. After a loss, everything *looks* the same, but the world becomes a totally different place. And there you are—stuck, sick to your stomach, and more stuck. The world's a blank, the future's a blank. You're living in a slow-motion hell with a pretend smile stapled to your face.

"How about we go camping?" I asked the girls over our morning eggs.

They had been camping in the Catskills, but this time, we would go all the way to the Pacific Northwest. Oregon, Washington State, California; after seeing how their faces brightened, I knew it was the right decision. A trip like this would give us football fields of freedom to grieve. Away from everything, we'd owe nothing to anyone, or ourselves. It would just be me and the girls, spending sunny days in fields of wildflowers or walking for miles on overcast beaches, where we'd trace the letters of his name into the sand until the tides came in.

I could picture it all so vividly, traced in soft watercolors and smiles. We would come across a wild blueberry bush and lay in the grass eating berries until the bush was bare, then jump in a rocky pool under a waterfall for a late afternoon swim before lighting a giant campfire. We would stare up at the stars, sometimes not seeing a soul or saying a word for hours.

And along the way, we would prove to ourselves that we *were* capable and that we *were* strong and that we *could* survive and do it alone. *All* of it. I made a little list.

First, they needed to see mountains that were taller than their 6'4" father. Then we would hike them. Each of us would get three complaints a day. After that, it was time's up. I also needed to face my fears (heights, open water, dogs, being alone in the woods, driving in unfamiliar places since I can't read a map) *and* overcome them. We needed to remain optimistic and open-minded to deal with death and other life blows in as positive a way as possible. That meant eating a lot of ice cream!

They would need to have a strong belief in something bigger than themselves, be it God or Buddha or what have you now that their father was gone. We would talk a lot about life and what is expected of them in living by the golden rule. We would volunteer to help others and be a part of that group.

It went on. They needed to surround themselves with positive role models, exercise their bodies, read lots of books, learn to trust their guts, and to live in good conscience.

I wanted them to find meaning in their father's death and use it to move forward in their lives.

If I could teach them all that, then in the future they would be able to say, "So what about that messy breakup! I've hiked mountains or zip lined across canyons bigger than him!" Or, "I know how to build a campfire without lighter fluid! Of *course* I can nail that job interview." And, "Do you really think that is a good way to treat the situation? How would that make you feel?" And whenever grief came calling, they could cut it down to size in one karate chop to the knees! "Take *that,* you tear-jerking monster. You think I'm gonna let you stand in the way of my life? Kung-fu *you!*"

I wanted that kind of strength, that *resilience.* I wanted it for me, and I wanted it for my girls.

So that's what we would do. We would go far away from bills and death certificates and his business suits and the hallway outside our bedrooms where he died. We would seek new sights. We would have new adventures. We would get stronger and better.

This was a case of Magical Thinking that I was going to *make sure* came true.

My mother thought this was all a very bad idea. For starters, I might not come home to a job, she pointed out. Then what?

Well, Mom, I guess we'll starve to death and die.

She always tried to talk me out of doing whatever *big* thing I wanted to do, which, of course, only made me want to do it more.

In retrospect, I guess that's why I ran the idea past her first—to make me want to do it more. To make me feel like a rebellious teenager again. To make me angry enough to fight for something I wasn't really sure I wanted or could even do, until someone doubted me.

"How can you possibly take those girls camping by yourself, especially across the country?" she demanded. "It is so unsafe. You can't do this by yourself, Laura. You just *can't.*"

Here it comes.

"Why don't you come here instead?" she suggested, as though the idea had just occurred to her whereas I knew she had been waiting to suggest it for months. "Take a week off, not a month. Bring the girls to the neighborhood pool and relax in the sun all day if you want to."

I love my mom, but sometimes she just doesn't get me.

Granted, even my friends—the ones who *do* get me—didn't love the idea.

"Really? By yourself? Out west? I'd never do that," Kim worried, giving me the "Are you sure?" look.

Yes, I was sure.

And best of all, we would be surrounded by strangers, not the people who knew us and loved us and worried about us. Because that's what happens. People worry about the grievers. "Did she look pale today?" they ask. "Did they take their vitamins?" "What about the garbage? It's Monday, you know; are the cans on the curb?"

And then they check in on you, asking you how you're doing as they rub your arm or try to give you a hug. They mean well—and I really appreciated the love and care—but I came to hate hugs. They made me feel weak at a time when I needed to feel strong.

25

Mark-in-a-Box

"This rite of passage phenomenon, American youth have been hung up with since Kerouac. Whether it was just road fever or feeling boxed in, I had to get out of town. The next week I sold my electric guitar for half of what it was worth and set off for the Pacific Northwest."

—Excerpted from Mark's journals

My request for time off work was granted. Ms. M was more than happy to ship me off to Oregon (or anywhere far away, for that matter). I'm sure she said yes in hopes I'd fall off a mountain or simply drive off the road or change my mind about coming back to work.

The next trip to the deli was for the morning papers and to tell Deli Man the good news.

"It's something changed with you," he said, locking eyes with me the way he always did. While his English made me laugh, the way he looked straight through me didn't.

He told me I seemed lighter, if not happier. "What is up?" he asked.

I was bursting to tell him but at that moment decided not to for fear that he would get too excited and try to give me a hug, and the last thing I needed was affirmation from Mr. Deli Guru Man, with his "insightful insights" and cinnamon gum breath.

After a polite chat, I went straight home to eat our celebratory ice cream with Mark-in-a-box while searching the Internet for cool places to take the girls. That's when it hit me—how could we possibly leave him home alone? Sure, I left him for a few hours here and there, and that one overnight at Christmas, but not for an entire month. What if something happened, like the house catching on fire? No one would know to save him.

I knew he wasn't "real," but he was still my husband who just happened to live in a box on a bookshelf. I loved him no matter what, and I took care of him, dusting his box, sharing my day with him, taking him to bed at night, sometimes taking him outdoors for some fresh air or to run errands.

Even the thought of leaving Mark behind left me feeling panicky and nervous. Forget it, I decided. We can't go and leave Daddy home alone.

But how to bring him with us? Delta's rules do allow for cremains on a plane, but there was no way I was putting him in cargo. What if he got rerouted to Turkey? Could I bring him as carry-on? He only weighed eleven pounds, after all, and wouldn't need his own seat.

The answer was yes, and all it took was a death certificate. But what if something happened to him while we were camping? I worried. What if we dropped him and his ashes spread all over the ground or what if we somehow lost him. Then what?

Finally, I hit on the perfect solution! My Mark-in-a-Box would become Mark-in-Two-Boxes! I would leave half of him at home for safekeeping and bring the rest of him with us.

Now we had a plan...of sorts.

26

Just Breathe

"Perhaps it was my logic getting in the way
again, Buddha man. I'll meditate. I'll
breathe with conscious breath. I'll take it
in and breathe it out. Slow and steady like.
Therefore I am. Being. Just being."

—Excerpted from Mark's journals

I learned conscious calming and breathing techniques after ending up in the emergency room not once but twice, terrified I was dying from an attack of one kind or another. Asthma, heart, stroke, aneurysm. Perhaps all four at once?

"LAURA!" the doctor had called loudly to startle me out of it. It was the same hospital, the same emergency room Mark had gone to. I could even see Trauma Room E-330 down the hall, though Mark's doctor thankfully was not there that day. "You've got to stop crying, please, or I can't listen to your heart. Okay, that's better," she said, putting her hand on my shoulder as she moved the stethoscope front to back.

She was nice. I liked her.

She began running through the standard questions. "Are you having discomfort, tightness, uncomfortable pressure, fullness, squeezing in the center of the chest?"

"Yes," I said, "It really hurts."

"Does it last more than a few minutes, or does it come and go?"

"It's always there. It hardly ever goes away."

"Is it crushing chest pain?"

"Yes, but sometimes it hurts so much I feel like I could die."

"Is there pressure or pain that spreads to the shoulders, neck, upper back, jaw, or arms?"

"YES! AM I HAVING A HEART ATTACK?"

"I don't think so," she replied calmly. "Are you dizzy or experiencing nausea?"

"I feel like I'm going to pass out any second. And throw up."

"Are you getting clammy sweats, heart flutters, or paleness?"

"Yes. It's awful. I shake and sweat."

"Do you have shortness of breath and difficulty breathing?"

"It's like my body forgets to breathe."

Wait here, she told me, calling for an EKG. About twenty minutes later, she re-appeared in the doorway with the results. She looked at my chart, then at me. Then back to the chart. Then back to me. By then she knew this was my second time in the ER for the same thing, meaning whatever it was hadn't killed me...yet.

"How long ago?" she asked gently. She must have seen the box for "widowed" checked on the intake form.

"Thanksgiving."

"I'm so sorry," she said. I could tell she meant it. "Look at me. You're okay. You're having a panic attack, *not* a heart attack." Then she handed me a pill: Xanax. "Take this and call a friend to come get you. You are not dying, even though panic attacks can make you feel like you are. I get them sometimes, too, working here. You're grieving. It's tough work to get through it, but you will...Just breathe."

Before I could ask if it's possible to die from a broken heart, she had gone on to another patient.

That's okay; I can do my own research. And yes, it turns out you can: you can experience a cardiac consequence of grief called broken heart syndrome or stress-induced cardiomyopathy. It's characterized by sudden, intense chest pain and shortness of breath in reaction to a surge of stress hormones after extreme emotional or physical stress.

Easy, Laura. Conscious breathing, remember? Is your breathing relaxed, rhythmic, silent, and deep? Now extend the exhale...that's it. It will be okay. You will get through it. Just breathe.

I skipped the pill.

27

Up, Up, and Away

"A coincidence is in the eye of the beholder.
Or its maker. Danger is one thing. Meeting
eye to eye is another."

—Excerpted from Mark's journals

Getting through the flight from JFK to Portland International called for two things: conscious breathing and a book on amazing human survival stories. *Seriously, how bad could a panic attack be compared to, say, this guy, who saw the fin, felt the burning chomp, and started screaming, "There's a shark on my leg!"*

Just before he was pulled underwater, the flight attendant came by.

"Sure, we'd love some sparkling water and peanuts. Right, girls?" I played it cool, pretending that everything was A-OK in row 15, that I wasn't freaking out and about to die like the man in the book. And the girls *were* sitting there, happily reading their own books, so all I had to do was breathe and remember to keep it relaxed, rhythmic, silent, and deep.

I finally started to calm down around the chapter where someone else was having a serious encounter with an elephant. *That's a stressful situation*, I thought as I sat there reading about his attack while popping peanuts in my mouth. Poor guy couldn't outrun the stampeding elephant and, oh no, look out! The tusk went right through his thigh!

It only took six hours (or roughly 31,200 heart beats) before we were hugging my friend Bridget, with whom we would be staying for a few days before renting a car and camping gear.

One of our first adventures in Portland would be taking an organized group bike tour of the Columbia River Gorge. Bridget asked her assistant to sign us up, but then immediately wished she hadn't.

"Did I just hear you say the name Ben Bernanke?" I asked the young woman after she hung up the phone with her tour organizer friend.

As if on cue, she took a measured sip of her Iced Half-Caff Ristretto Venti 4-Pump Sugar Free Soy Skinny Latte—or something equally downtown Oregonian-like—before she spoke.

"Yeah. Like, why?" she asked, swirling the offending brew in her eco-friendly bamboo cup. (This is a common coffee drinking practice, I've noticed. Sip. Swirl. Sip. Swirl...) "He's one of the dudes on your tour."

"Ben Bernanke, as in the chairman of the Federal Reserve, Ben Bernanke, is the dude on our bike tour?"

"Yeah, why? Am I supposed to know who he is? Is he like a celebrity or something?"

I turned to address Bridget. "That's who Mark sued in the Bloomberg lawsuit!"

Before she could speak, I plowed on, wrecking any chance of going on the tour.

"Oh my God! Ben Bernanke is on the bike tour? Seriously? What am I going to do? I know, I'm going to tell him off the *second* I see him. I'm going to go straight up to him and say, 'Hey, Ben. You don't know me, but I'm Mark Pittman's widow. You know the name, right? Mark Pittman?' And then I'll watch his face fall and he'll be stuck feeling really guilty and uncomfortable and he'll have no choice but to help the girls ride their bikes up the big hills or give them his last bottle of water while he dies of thirst. Maybe he'll even feel so guilty that he'll treat them to ice cream afterwards. How 'bout that? Huh?"

I hadn't noticed just how crazy I must have sounded. I *also* hadn't noticed the assistant quietly leave the room to arrange to remove us from the tour.

By the time we got to the bike shop, the van had "just left," with Bernanke on it.

"You mean they left without us?" I asked the young bearded man running the shop. He looked up from where he knelt fiddling with a bike chain and spoke just four words: "Do you blame them?" That's when I fully understood that I had been blocked. De-friended. Thumbs downed.

That's when I called Bob, Mark's writing partner in New York.

"Can you believe it? Ben Bernanke, in the flesh! And I blew it! Totally blew it! I am *such* an idiot! I could've *had* him! But no—I go and hyperventilate in front of everybody to the point where they pulled me off the tour!" I told Bob on the phone.

"Holy crap! That's crazy! Unbelievable!" I could almost see him jumping up and down in the newsroom the way he and Mark often did. "Maybe Pittman is up there after all!"

"Yeah, maybe," I thought. "Maybe he really is..."

After the bike tour incident, I decided it was time to s...l...o...w... down.

BE...BE...BE—that was my new mantra.

BE—BE the mountain you see over there.

BE—BE the sunshine you feel on your shoulders.

BE—BE the bottle of Kaopectate.

By the time I BE'd needing medication, I knew we had worn out our welcome at Bridget's.

Thankfully, it was our last day. Susannah had already played with—and promptly lost—our hostess' stainless steel tweezers, the ones in the fancy leopard print case she had picked up at a museum gift shop. Bridget handled it graciously, but there are always plenty of annoyances that come with having two children invade your space.

For our last meal together before leaving, Bridget suggested that we "go in on" a $70 piece of "freshly caught" salmon, which was apparently already ice-packed and en route to her doorstep as if being rushed by ambulance off the chef's fishing boat. I sheepishly declined; even if this were in my budget, everyone with kids knows they *hate* fish. They won't eat it, not on their lives.

We decided on family dinner at IKEA where we could "dine" on 99-cent Swedish meatball platters. Kids *do* love Swedish meatballs. It was a good call before heading off into the woods.

28
Tastes Like Chicken

"I'm living dreams dreamt a thousand miles away. Landlocked Kansas boy in rut on sand dunes, waves crash, and the smell of rotting surf drifts. I think maybe she's got something to do with it."

—Excerpted from Mark's journals

If there's one thing I'm really bad at, it's assembling anything that comes with directions—especially tents. Mark could have easily pitched this baby one-handed, yet I couldn't do it with two (six, if you count my enthusiastic nine- and eleven-year-olds).

Nell had taken the lead having already read the setup instructions by way of the car headlights. She told me not to worry, she knew just what to do. Susannah helped by handing us the poles and ties.

"Build the greater poles by pushing the shock-corded segments together until each pole is complete," Nell instructed, looking at her sister and me expectantly, if not impatiently.

I had no idea what a shock cord segment was, and we couldn't find anything that looked like one, either. After twenty minutes of struggling, we high-fived each other for a job poorly done, climbed inside the half-pitched roof, and conked out. It was either that, or call the Mountain Shop begging for help.

What was that?

It had sounded like a baby crying—long, plaintive wails, followed by strange gurgling noises. *Maybe it's a lost, hungry baby*, I dreamt, *crawling around in its Pampers looking for a jar of pureed peas.*

I tried to fall back asleep, burying myself deeper inside the sleeping bag's warm blue cocoon. It was only our first night, with about thirty more to go. I couldn't let a few woodland babies keep me from a good night's sleep.

A few minutes later, the noise startled me awake again.

Waaah...*Grrr...*

Okay, now I was scared, *really* scared; as in, too scared to pack up and pull my family out of there.

I sat still, listening to the silence, readying to kill whatever was coming to get us *before* it came and got us. I had it all planned: first, I pop out of the tent, which would scare the crap out of it (whatever *it* was). Then, I would clock it over the head with the lantern until it blacked out, then spray it in the face with the fire extinguisher, making sure to send plenty of foam straight up its nostrils.

Waaah...*Grrr...*

If this thing got any closer, I would be able to smell its putrid breath, count its snaggly fangs and see the red cast of its veiny eyes.

This was all Deli Man's fault, I decided. *He had read the wrong mind!*

When I heard it again, that's when I realized the noise was *not* coming from outside the tent.

It was coming from me.

Clutching my stomach, I knew I had to move quickly, gasping out a quick "thank you" to IKEA for their meatballs continuing service. Have a nice day; more like, have a nice diarrhea.

There were two choices: either "go" over by a nearby tree or "go" further out, to the outhouse. I had to do some quick thinking; I knew if I ran Olympian fast, I could *probably* make it to the toilet in time (though "toilet" was being a bit kind), but that would mean leaving the girls alone, asleep in the tent. *What if they woke up scared because I was gone? Or what if the outhouse itself were not an outhouse at all, but a trap? What if a toothless killer in red flannel lurked inside, ready to stuff my mouth with Charmin and drag my muffled body into the woods to chop me into salmon chum?*

It could happen, ya know.

The outhouse wasn't doing much to help, sitting there all alone out there in the middle of a field. Still, the thought of doing you-know-what outside and having to cover it up like a dog was almost worse than braving the walk. It was certainly more disgusting.

This was only our first night, and I was already regretting my earlier logic of, "I love camping, so I'll be really good at it."

That's when I realized something. I didn't *have* to go to the outhouse alone. Mark-in-a Box could come and protect me.

Meanwhile, it was doo-doo or die time. Squeezing my cheeks (you know which ones) together with one hand, Mark-in-a-Box and a flashlight in the other, I began trotting toward the outhouse. Only I somehow tripped over my own feet and landed, splat! Grit filled my mouth. *Great*, I thought. I had face-planted into the fire pit. Now, in addition to everything else, I was covered in ash.

That's when I realized I was nowhere near the fire pit.

The ash was from Mark. I mean, it *was* Mark. His box must have broken open in the fall.

As I frantically scraped at the ground, trying to dust him up, my hands ran over pieces of metal, screws and some things that resembled pen springs—remnants from his ankle fusion and stent surgeries. That could only mean one thing—that those hard white things on the ground and in my mouth were chunks of bone.

But I still didn't spit him out. I swallowed him. Because that's what you do when you love someone, right? You swallow their bones.

Lying back in my tent a few minutes later, staring out at the star filled sky, I wondered if maybe this wasn't a coincidence at all. Maybe Mark had waited until the perfect moment to let me know he wanted out—OUT OF HIS BOX! And not necessarily just here, at this campground. It was there at that moment the idea came to me. Maybe I could pick out all the places he would want to go and sprinkle a bit of his ashes at each location.

"Girls, let's go hike that mountain and bring Daddy with us," I suggested, dipping into the box when they weren't looking.

After last night, I knew he would be dying to get out of his box to stretch his legs a bit more.

Sprinkle...

The high afternoon sun shone down on the now ash-dusted rock. Out in nature like that, he blended in perfectly, not much different from any other organic matter. Still, it was startling to see those bits of bone in daylight, to recognize that his legs would never again carry him up or down another mountain.

He needed us for that now.

The next day, just as the sun was gearing up to burst through the purple dawn on the beach, I reached into the box again.

Mark disappeared in the sand, washing out with the waves, tumbling and swirling in the foamy water. I stood there, tracing his trail until he was gone...

Easy, Laura. Conscious breathing, remember? Is your breathing relaxed, rhythmic, silent and deep? Now extend the exhale...that's it. It will be okay. You will get through it. Just breathe.

In return for the earth accepting him, I took a handful of dirt from wherever I released him and mixed it in with his ashes. Through this exchange, I could keep Mark alive and take part of his new homes with me.

At first, I was careful not to let the girls know. "It's only another mile," I called back to them on another hiking trail above the Pacific Ocean as they stopped to look for bugs under rocks. I skipped ahead, my sights set on the treetops, where Mark would have a nice view of the ocean for centuries to come.

Sprinkle...

The next day, I secretly sprinkled him by a really cool bike in an Auto Zone parking lot. At that moment, I wished so badly that he had told me more about the motorcycle trip he took during college. All I really remember is he went with a guy named Wily.

"Look at that big motorcycle, Mommy," Nell said just as I released the ashes under the tire. "Didn't he have one, too? Is that the same kind?"

This was her way of letting me know, "Hey, Mom, do you have a minute? I need to talk about my father."

So we sat down, right there on the sidewalk, to do just that: to talk about their father.

"Daddy always loved to feel the wind in his hair," I told the girls. Translation: He drove without a helmet. "And I'm not really sure where he went or what he did, just that he told me it changed his life."

The girls' smiles were as wide as the handlebars, especially when the owner and his wife let them sit on the bikes and start the engines.

We stuck close to the Pacific Coast Scenic Byway, better known as U.S. Route 101. It was a major north-south route, with no east or west; just a beautiful two-lane undivided highway, with mountains on one side and the Pacific Ocean on the other. *How could we possibly get lost?*

Let me tell you, easily, especially when there were no warnings about the landslides. (Yes, you heard right, *landslides*; as in, when part of a mountain slides off onto the road after excessive rainfall.) We found out the hard way, in the dark. The big orange and white flashing sign indicating "detour" was the first notification that something was wrong ahead.

The GPS lady just kept saying that she had "lost satellite reception." *Now what?* I guess I could drive until I found something, anything, but it was remarkably desolate out there. Who could say how long it would take to find someone to direct us, and whether it would be in some creepy gross meth town?

Turn around, Laura. That's the best thing to do. Always listen to your gut, I say.

We found a Best Western hotel about fifty miles back. A quick sprinkle in the parking lot...an exhalation of relief...and we were safe.

For now, at least. So far, no one caught me with my hand in the box, but it was only a matter of time before one of them saw me do it. Then what? I knew it was better to ask if they would be comfortable with it rather than risk them freaking out, but how to bring it up?

Over lunch, I decided.

"Uh...so, girls," I began. *But how do you introduce a subject like this?* "What would you think if I told you that, while we've been hiking, I've been sprinkling some of Daddy's ashes in really pretty places in nature, like off that waterfall? Would you think that was gross or weird?"

"Oh, you mean like mini-funerals?" Nell asked.

"That's a good way of looking at it," I said, seizing on my daughter's interpretation. "Yes, like mini-funerals."

Susannah smiled. "I think it's really cool, Mom. I bet he'd really like that. It's way better than being crammed in that tiny little box for the rest of his life."

"Susannah..." Nell said. "I hate to tell you this, but Daddy's dead. That's why he lives in the box in the first place. Otherwise, he'd be sitting here eating your French fries."

It's true; he would have. Susannah was probably the only kid in the world who hated French fries. But the thought of him not being able to eat her fries anymore was more than we could handle.

"Don't worry sweetheart," I told her, wiping her tear-filled eyes with my sleeve. "I'll eat your fries from now on. I promise. See? Look. I'm eating them now."

She hugged me while glaring at her sister. "Okay, Mom. Thanks."

Both wanted to be first to sprinkle him.

"How about here?" Susannah called out from alongside a blue taco truck. We had finished lunch when the truck just happened to pull out of its parking spot. "Daddy loved Mexican food."

And with that, she reached her small hand into the box and sprinkled a handful on the ground. Some people might think that's sick, but to me, it was a beautiful acceptance of our role in helping him to live a good death.

"My turn," Nell said excitedly as we walked into a Barnes & Noble, where she put a pinch inside her favorite book, *Alice in Wonderland*.

"I loved the part where Daddy pretended to be Absolem the caterpillar when he'd read it to me. He'll like it there. I know he will, Mom."

By now, the trip had taken on new meaning. It had purpose now, a big, meaningful purpose. Sometimes, we held hands in the middle of a golden field while releasing him to the wind and they saw my tears; sometimes, I saw theirs.

Other times weren't so ceremonious, but then they would make up for it by taking turns leading us in "prayer sprinkles" where they would talk to God. This always reminded me of the backyard ceremony Mark had officiated when their gerbil died.

"Dear God," he preached, holding the girls' hands to form a circle around the little grave that he carefully dug. "We are gathered here today to remember Pepper, the best gerbil in the whole, wide world," he started. Before I knew it, he started to read from the Bible his grandmother had given him as a young boy.

When he finished the passage, I elbowed him sharply in the side. "Don't you think you're taking this a little too far, honey?" I asked.

Apparently not; he proceeded to go on for a good ten minutes, preaching to the girls about the importance of family, doing the right thing in life, and serving mankind while we stood together under the big western white pine tree in our backyard. There were actual tears forming in his eyes.

"Mark, it was a freaking gerbil. It's not like a person died. Why are you acting like this?" I whispered tersely. "What is wrong with you?"

The answer came four days later. That's when he died: four days later.

"Dear God," Nell intoned, looking up toward the sky, "please tell my father—his name is Mark Pittman—that I really miss him and that I hope he's having fun on our trip."

"Daddy, can you see me? Look. It's me, Susannah. I'm right here! Hi, Daddy! We miss you."

29

Johnny-Come-Lately

"A sign a couple of hundred miles down the
road warned of flash floods. While there was
no real reason to doubt it, that sign was
the closest thing this area's had for rain
in years. It was cold. His breath blew in
long plumes over his flannelled arms, feet
stepping high in foot-deep mud."

—Excerpted from Mark's journals

After a few weeks of coastal exploring, camping, and now
sprinkling, we headed to the airport. John had flown out last
minute to join us—the consummate enabler, he was the Ethel to my
Lucy.

"Set the table, Lucy," he said when he had heard Mark died. I
knew what that meant; the table is where John, his wife Rachel, Mark,
and I had spent endless hours forming a lifelong friendship over
grilled steaks and bottles of wine.

It was also where John and I hatched any number of "Lucy
Schemes" over the years. Start an organic vegetable delivery service
called "Peace, Love, Vegetables?" Genius. Buy investment properties
and flip them? Sure, let's be real estate developers. How about

fabricating X-rated miniature golf course sculptures on rooftops in Miami, Vegas, and L.A.?

If it weren't for my dragging John along with my, "Oh, we'll find our way, it'll be fun to go exploring, join us for part of the trip" logic, I'm not sure what I would have done.

Mark-in-a-Box or no Mark-in-a-Box, it was *scary*—at least at that fragile point in life—to be in charge of anything *and* to be responsible for its outcome.

"This is going to be our best adventure yet, Lucy," he declared happily as the girls ran up to hug him.

"Mom, look! He's here! John's here! Now we're really going to have fun!"

At first, I didn't tell him about the sprinkles, sprinkles, sprinkles when he wasn't looking, looking, looking. But pretty soon, I couldn't wait to let him in on the expedition's new purpose. I knew that if anyone had something to say about this, it would be John.

The conversation went something like this:

"So...what do you think?"

"Are you kidding me?" he asked. "Who *wouldn't* love this, especially Pittman? This beats visiting a depressing graveyard; I think this may just be your best Lucy yet!"

And so off we went, taking turns closing our eyes and pointing to a spot on the map, letting fate set our itinerary. We started in Reedsport then got an ocean view campground in Florence, Oregon. The Tillamook Cheese Factory had a good guided tour for cheese lovers and then it was down Three Capes Scenic Drive where Mark enjoyed a few sprinkles out the window. In Pacific City, a nice fisherman agreed to sprinkle Mark by the famous Haystack Rock; he's in the fireplace at the famous Timberline Lodge and at the top of Mount Bachelor, where I swore I'd never mount another bachelor again. He's at Government Camp (we sincerely apologize for leaving without paying); at Warm Spring Indian Reservation where he now sleeps on a feather bed in one of the historical reenactment rooms... The list goes on and on. He became part of a traveling magician troupe when Nell got pulled on stage to be sawed in half; and he was particularly active in the city of Bend, where he went biking up the Cascade Mountains and fly fishing in my waders before I took him skinny dipping under the stars in Diamond Lake as John pitched our tents.

Of course we ignored the weather forecast, warning folks about an overnight thunderstorm and possible flash floods. And now, of course, we were knee-deep in it.

"John!" I shouted. When he didn't answer, I worried that he died in his sleep, until there came the unmistakable sound of a man snoring.

"John, wake up!" I yelled again, this time shaking his tent, not realizing the whole soggy thing would collapse on top of him.

"John! Get up! The campground is underwater!"

"Lucy?! What have you done?" he called out, startled, as he struggled against the tent like a trapped bug.

Hauling our heavy water- and mud-logged sleeping bags and other assorted equipment into the minivan, I promised myself to never go camping again.

We were shivering. We were exhausted. We were dirty. And we were hungry. That's when we checked into our first motel since the landslides. A Howard Johnson's, I think; all that mattered was it had steamy hot water, scented soap, and real beds with clean sheets.

Each night, when the adventures were finished, and we had found a place to lay under the stars, the girls and I cuddled in our sleeping bags together. It was us against nature, and it felt good to be alive.

"Mom, why did Dad have to die? Why couldn't a robber or someone bad die instead?" Susannah asked one night.

"I wish I knew, honey. It doesn't seem fair that someone bad gets to live and someone good had to die, but that's life. It's hard for you, I know...but just try to remember all the fun things you did together and how much he loved you. That will keep him close to you. He doesn't want you to feel sad and only think about that night. But we can talk about that, too, if you want."

Her big, sleepy brown eyes got bigger, as if she had a wonderful idea. "Do you think he's watching us from heaven? Can he see us?"

This was exactly what I wanted from this trip—time alone and away with the girls to have these types of conversations without the rush of school and work and household activities to distract us from ourselves. Out here, the girls wouldn't see their friends waiting with their fathers at the bus stop together, getting hugs and kisses goodbye. No one would ask how they were doing. The conversations would not be forced; they'd form like dew on morning leaves.

Watching them take in the beautiful scenery, play in the water and scramble up the rocks as fast as they could, was all the proof I needed. This was the right thing to do for them, for Mark. And for me.

With that, I kissed her forehead as she lay peacefully sleeping.

30

Rock Bottom

"Sometimes you can realize immediately when you're at the crossroads. A choice this way or that, and your life has taken a different direction. Sometimes all it takes is a U-turn."

—Excerpted from Mark's journals

Our biggest schemes are hatched in a moment of impulse decision-making.

"Do you see what I see?" I asked John excitedly. (We were now in Sequim, Washington, the "Lavender Capital of North America.") I knew he saw it, too. His expression was at once electrified and almost terrified.

"Oh, Lucy. Are you serious?" He lifted his sunglasses to look in my eyes, as if that would change my mind. The sign for Peninsula RV Sales reflected off the lenses.

Too late. "Don't try to talk me out of it," I warned. "Pull a U-ey! If that thing is under $5,000, I'm buying it!"

I got the RV salesman down to $4,200, and soon became the proud owner of a 1993 Toyota Dolphin, a fully equipped, self-contained freewheeling motorhome. It was a class C vehicle, which means there's a loft bed above the driver and passenger seats, where the girls would sleep together, or else they could take turns sleeping with me. The bed compartment came complete with wooden sconce reading lights. Score! No more reading by flashlight. It had two single beds that doubled as couches, one of which split in half to prop up the kitchen table. No more waking up with a log poking out of your back; no more pitching tents in the dark. It had a refrigerator, a stove with four gas burners, an oven, a microwave, and a double sink. But that's not all! A stand-up shower? Check. Toilet? Check. Closet and clothing compartments? Check; no more hanging your wet clothes in the trees to dry! No more backpacks either.

Plus, it was purple and white—our two favorite colors.

A quick calculation (somewhat biased by desire) determined that this baby would pay for itself quickly when you factor in the cost of motels, campsites, restaurant dining, outdoor supplies, and more.

A signed loan agreement and a fill-up with gas later, we were now a part of the new subculture of Costco and Walmart-loving RVers. We, too, wanted to "simplify home and life" and "spend less and live better." Where else could we go inside wearing pajamas and come out munching on organic apples? Oh, and don't forget the Fritos and onion dip! Or the amazing pizza and hot dogs! Really, how can you expect anyone to refuse all the free samples? They're actually encouraged! And when you get down to it, if someone is giving you food at every turn, from bits of chocolate to ravioli on pieces of wax paper, you're ready to be their best friend forever—especially if the store doesn't mind you snacking while watching an Oprah rerun on one of their high definition TVs! We were sold.

And so was HaRVey, who got in on the action with new blinds and curtains, purple sheets and fluffy pillows, windshield wiper fluid, a spare tire, and everything he needed to provide a fully equipped kitchen, including shelf organizers. He also needed a new car radio which they installed while we waited.

The new overall look? One part Martha Stewart to two parts Cheech and Chong.

But really, the best home decorating purchase—the pièce de résistance—was a pink shag carpet steering wheel cover that would become my spiritual guide.

I don't know whether it was the comfort of the RV itself or having made such a major, unexpected change in our plans—or maybe it was just that we had a new groove—but my heart immediately felt lighter.

Driving the RV was easier than I thought, and soon we became more like road warrior adventurers than burdened pilgrims. Even the sprinklings became less tearful, more empowering.

"That was awesome!" Susannah exclaimed one day after an exhilarating kayak trip with their father. It was the girls' first time, and while they had been slightly afraid at first, both took to it like pro paddlers. "I never thought we'd make it past those rocks and the wavy part, but we did!"

As we lay picnicking on the water's edge, Susannah pulled up a big blade of grass, pursed it perfectly between her lips, and made it whistle.

What a day! It was full of exactly what we needed to be doing—a lot of everything and a lot of nothing. It was just us; we could spend the day learning how to kayak or whistling in a field of grass if that's what we wanted to do.

Sprinkle…(in fact, make it three!)

"Let's take Daddy horseback riding so he can be a cowboy again!" Nell suggested.

While this was a great way to connect with him, I had to balance out the adventures by staying within our budget. We would often fill in our days with lots of free activities like fishing or sightseeing and eating boxed mac and cheese.

This time, however, I decided to splurge on the overnight horseback camping trip up the Grand Teton mountains in Jackson

Hole, Wyoming. The girls were ahead of me, as usual, but for once, it wasn't fear holding me back. It was the horse. It wouldn't move. I tried talking to it. No response. I tried giving it a little kick. It pooped. How about feeding it a carrot seasoned with a peppering of ashes?

Cassidy was now in the lead.

But whenever a sprinkling got really tough, like it did on that mountain top for some reason, John would tell redneck RV jokes to sidetrack the tears.

"How do you know when you're a redneck, Lucy?" he would ask, smiling. Then he'd rattle off clever punchlines:

"When you have to change the oil on your house every 3,000 miles.

"When going to the bathroom in the middle of the night requires shoes, a jacket, and a flashlight.

"If you had a toothpick in your mouth when you had your wedding picture taken."

The girls had quickly decided our redneck ride needed a name.

Daisy? Nah, too girly.

Star? Maybe.

The Lobster Crusher? No one would get it but us.

"How about HaRVey?" Susannah suggested. That was it! We'd name him HaRVey! And now, we had a new addition to the family.

Before HaRVey set us on our new path, I had planned to return the rental car at the end of the month and simply fly back. But Mark's desires were not to be denied, and neither were mine. Now we could spread him everywhere: not just Oregon, but California, Washington State, Idaho, Montana, Wyoming...all the way home to New York.

Now we had a plan. An even *bigger* plan!

31

Dumpster Diving

"It was as if life's vital source had been
sucked from earth. My feet lost grounding.
I was deep in and I knew it. There was no
getting out."

—Excerpted from Mark's journals

Of course, no plan is perfect. Even John was helpless to console me when we lost Mark. Correction: when he got thrown away in a McDonald's garbage can on an Indian reservation in Oregon.

The last time I sprinkled him was at the Pike Place Market in Seattle, where he had enjoyed swimming in a vase full of giant sunflowers. Susannah had been standing lookout for me, happily eating a big juicy peach, until ten minutes later when her face blew up in a bright red, puffy allergic reaction. I gave her Benadryl which prompted a sleep-induced face-plant right into her chicken salad shortly afterwards.

That day I learned three important things. First, that Susannah had developed an allergy to anything with pits in it—even though her last name was Pittman. This meant no more peaches, avocados, cherries, plums, nada. Second, that Benadryl knocks her right out, and is enough to make her fall asleep mid-meal, even one in a nice restaurant. And third, you should never take unfinished chicken salad home in a doggie bag. It may cause you to lose your husband.

"Where's Mark?" I called out from the front seat.

John's face registered both anguish and fright.

"What do you mean, where's Mark?"

"I don't know. He was right here and now he's gone!" I began searching under the gray travel pal—that plastic thing that goes in between the front seats with a place for everything, from spare change to coffee cups. Or in this case, a box of ashes. John began ripping through the cabinets and looking under the seats, clothes and books scattering, while I woke the girls up to help with the search.

An RV's living space is only about 40 sq. feet. What that means is, if you can't find something within seconds, it's surely gone.

"Hello, McDonald's," said the voice on the phone. We had stopped there for a cup of coffee and to do a quick clean up of HaRVey.

"Hi," I said, "This is a serious problem. My husband's ashes got accidentally thrown out in the trash cans in front of your restaurant."

The lady on the phone laughed. "Come on, who is this? Shoni?"

She soon realized I wasn't her friend Shoni at all, and immediately put her manager on the phone. (I didn't need to bypass pressing "1" to order fries or "2" for a chocolate shake to get him on the line either.

"Oh, man," he said, after hearing the whole story. "We've got a problem. The trash cans get dumped into the container out back at 8:30 every morning."

It was now close to 3:00 pm.

This was not good news. For him, I mean—the man on the phone. It meant one thing and one thing only—that he would either have to live with guilt for the rest of his life...or offer to go dumpster diving to find Mark.

"Can you...get him out?" I asked, wincing at the thought of someone digging through mounds of half-eaten slop in search of some guy's cremains.

"I don't see how I can do that," he hesitated.

"What's a little hamburger between your toes when you could save a life here?" I tried cajoling, only he didn't laugh. Or speak.

I knew what would get him to agree.

"Can you hold on, please?" I asked, making sure he could hear me say, "Girls, the man said he can't rescue your father."

There was a long silence.

"... Okay. Alright, I'll do it."

"You will? Really? Thank you!" I exclaimed. "Thank you so much! You won't regret it, I promise. Just take a nice hot shower when you get home. I'm more than happy to pay to have your uniform cleaned too if you want."

It took about forty agonizing minutes before the cell phone would ring again.

"We've got him! We found him! Your husband is here!" the manager called out, now bursting with excitement.

"Girls! John! McDonald's found Daddy! He really *was* in the dumpster!"

"Yeah!" they hugged, jumping up and down. "Daddy's back!"

The problem now was how to get Mark now that we were six hours away in Boise, Idaho. The good news was, we had a mailing address we could use (John had become fast friends with the owner of a local tattoo parlor owner); the bad news was the McDonald's manager told us it was illegal to mail ashes. He said they would keep Mark there for a day or two, tops; otherwise, it was implied that he would end up back in the dumpster where they found him.

Many phone calls later, I tracked down the chief of the Indian reservation on which the McDonald's was located, a man named Akecheta. He had heard about "the situation" and offered the perfect solution—to give Mark a full dress Indian burial service in a western white pine tree forest the next day.

In other words, he was taking this seriously...and ceremoniously.

But first, he wanted to explain his tribe's customs and talk to me about Mark in order to make a real connection with the man he was about to bury on his 10,000-year-old sacred land.

Their beliefs, as I learned, are core to their understanding or the nature of human existence—both during life and after death. The relations of the living to the dead are all recorded in their customs; that's why he spoke about the importance of future love for the departed, to make them become more wise and good after death. He told me that a spirit, if they are meant to connect with the living, often will do so even when no physical body is present; that individuals can come back in other forms if they have more "work" to do on earth.

Did that mean...

Was it possible that I was *wasn't* imagining feeling Mark's presence? That he had already been in certain places and was guiding me there to be with him again?

"I swear," I told Akecheta, "that I sometimes feel his presence. Like, he's here. You mean it's possible I'm not imagining that?"

"He's connecting with you and the girls, Laura, and he will always be connected to you, in this life and in others," he replied. "The spirit—Mark's spirit, your ancestors' spirits—are with you at all times. He may have lived before in another life or perhaps in a completely different time, but he is now here to be with you, to teach you, to guide you, to be with you on your journey through your own lives."

This is what happens when you take your husband's ashes on the road. You meet the kindest of strangers, people who will forever hold an incredibly important place in your heart and family's history and who will never be forgotten.

They are the teachers.

Mark's remaining ashes—the ones I left at home for safekeeping—arrived safely at the tattoo parlor a day later, courtesy of a friend back home who'd overnighted the package. Thankfully, Mark didn't go down while in his black box; we had taken a lot of him out to lunch that day in a black velvet pouch, the one we reserved for times where he needed to be dressed for an occasion.

Next stop? Yellowstone, where he and Old Faithful were reunited as one. Then it was onto Cody, Wyoming, where we tied a pair of elk horns to HaRVey's front grill for safety. Out there, in the Wild West, it's elk against man.

I-90 took us to Wall, South Dakota. It was hard to miss the world-famous American roadside Wall Drug Store, with its hundreds of billboards lining the highway, tantalizing travelers with offers of five-cent coffee and free ice water. Inside you'll find every tourist trinket imaginable, from soap holders to salt water taffy. Oh, and Mark, too. He's now out back with the life size T-Rex.

We then cruised down US Route 85 to Deadwood, where we sprinkled him like badass outlaws at 5 am, and then he got to meet Washington, Jefferson, Lincoln, and Roosevelt. He's also in the Badlands, which is where he really belongs.

The girls had been total troopers up to this point, taking each day as a new adventure as they bounced along from site to site, place to place, never knowing where we would land next—but everyone has their limits. They had begun bickering with each other in the way kids do, over whose turn it was to sit in the coveted front seat or who got to sleep on which side of the "big" bed.

"I never knew the world was so big," Nell told me, "but I really want to go to where it is small again."

"Me too, I'm homesick," Susannah agreed.

They were right. We were fried little monkeys. But we were still 1,526 miles from home.

Fast forward, past sprinkles in Okoboji, Iowa at a friend's lake house; Sioux Falls, Minnesota; Madison and La Crosse, Wisconsin; Chicago, Illinois, on home plate at Wrigley Field; off the Willis Tower Skydeck in the Chicago River; by the Inuit mask collection at the Field Museum of Natural History. We drove through Detroit, sprinkling him without stopping, then it was on to Cleveland's Chinatown (Mark loved dumplings) and straight through to Niagara Falls where Mark not only survived the falls, but also the Maid of the Mist.

As we sat down for our last supper together in one of those giant cafeterias on the final day of our trip, the universe provided a soundtrack.

There's this idea called "magical thinking." It refers to "a non-scientific or irrational belief centered on correlations between events;" in other words, the belief that there's no such thing as coincidences. And it may be unscientific and irrational, but when the piped-in elevator music abruptly stopped, and out of nowhere, Bob Dylan's raspy voice took over, singing Mark's funeral song, "Blowin' in the Wind"...

Well, what am I supposed to think?

While it was possible that only his left toe ended up in Montana, his heart in San Francisco, or one ear in Seattle and the other in Crater Lake, I hoped that his smile was still intact among the ashes, and that the girls and I could carry it with us wherever we went. But even if it's all mixed up together and spread from coast to coast, the truth is that we left little bits of ourselves in all those places too.

Albany was our last stop. It's where we said goodbye to John before returning to so-called real life in Yonkers which unfortunately included going back to school and work, and all the other tedious routines that make the end of summer hard to accept.

New to the mix, however, was figuring out how to deal with the month's worth of human waste that had been sloshing along with us from sea to shining sea in HaRVey's now *very* full toilet tank.

Seriously! How could anyone expect me to know how to maintain an RV, other than to gas it up and scrub bugs off the windshield? Otherwise I wouldn't have done what I did—unscrew the sewage cap thinking it was the water cap. In my defense, it was dark out and there was no one there to help, and it *was* the first time I had ever attempted to deal with the mechanics of what's apparently (and appropriately) called "black water."

Before going any further, let me state for the record that there was no poo involved—just 172 gallons of pee, reeking toilet paper, and dirty dish and shower water, flooding out of HaRVey straight onto the asphalt of the convenience store parking lot with the same thunderous force as Horseshoe Falls. Fearing arrest under any number of city and/or state environmental laws, I got out of there, *fast*, as HaRVey continued to leak a trail down the highway.

I suppose we all have to live with and answer for our own messes—if not on the road, then when we get back home.

Still, I would like to extend my sincere apologies to the people of that small town, which we left just a bit smellier than we had found it.

Part III:
When a House
Is Not a Home

32

Home Is Where the Heart Dies

"I came across many a lost traveler on the
road; we would connect for a brief, necessary
moment—to exchange directions, forecasts, or
hellos—and then go our separate ways. Other
times, we'd travel together for a period of
time, each representing nothing more than
passing mile markers to gauge our journeys."

—Excerpted from Mark's journals

"Ahh, so she returns!" Deli Man said cheerfully. I had forgotten to get eggs, milk, and cereal for the girls' breakfast.

"I have not seen you in weeks," Deli Man continued. "Did you go somewhere? To the beaches? To far away?"

He offered me a loosie, but I shook my head no.

"No more cigarettes?" he asked.

"Nope," I replied, "I haven't smoked in more than a month. I took your advice, or whatever you call it, and went camping out west."

"You did it? You went on vacation? *And* you stopped smoking? No wonder you look better! Put on some weight, look healthier; tan, too. For you, this was good. Very, very good."

I couldn't help but smile. This man, this almost-stranger, was really happy to have helped his "disciple." I told him a little about the trip—how we had climbed mountains, slept out under the stars, rode horses, went white water rafting, explored volcanoes—but didn't get into the rest of it. You know, the ashes and all of that.

"It did us good, just like you said."

"You feel good now, I can tell. Were there cowboys and Indians? Pocahontas?"

I had to laugh. It was funny; I hadn't thought about him on the trip and certainly didn't miss him, but I was surprisingly happier to see Deli Man than I'd expected. It was almost comforting to find him in the same place, wearing the same thing, standing behind the same cluttered counter, smiling the same happy smile. In a way, his continued presence represented a reassuring timestamp in life. A then and now. A "before and after" for the trip.

I almost...*hugged* him.

We had won our gold medals.

"Hi, honey! We're home!" I felt like shouting and beeping in celebration as we pulled in the driveway. Like, "See, Mark? Don't worry about us! We *are* okay! We *can* and *did* do this! The girls are doing *so much* better! Look at their little muscles and their tans! We became explorers! Adventurers! Conquerors! We *peed* in the woods!

It was all too exciting...until we walked in the front door. I had to squeeze my eyes closed, covering them with my hands to stop the flashbacks. Only it was too late; I could see *everything* I had blocked out, moving at me in fast motion. His body. The blood. The sirens. Everything.

I immediately threw up in the bushes.

It felt at once oddly familiar and also completely foreign. If this was our house and these were our things, why did I feel like a stranger standing in someone else's living room? Preparing to move forward isn't the same as actually moving forward, turns out.

I hoped the "doomy" feeling would pass once we got settled— whatever that meant. But for me, I knew the memories of that night would always be right there, camping out in the corners and making themselves comfortable on the furniture.

How was it possible that I had traveled more than 6,500 miles to end up right back where I started? I had finally reached the fifth and final stage of grief—Acceptance—or so I thought. And now here I was, back in the first stage, Denial.

I would love to say how we took all the accumulated wisdom and experience from our trip and used it to live more empowered and purposeful lives, or something equally uplifting...but that would be all too neat and pretty.

In truth, now that we were home, it was almost as if the trip and all its healing never happened.

33

Cemetery Hellos and Graveyard Goodbyes

"I've got this great place picked out.
Windswept hill lined with crosses with
a stump on top of the plot I'd picked...
shouldn't be hard digging there."

—Excerpted from Mark's journals

It sounds morbid, but one of my favorite places to walk the dog is in the graveyard down the street. It's always dead quiet (ha-ha...ha), there are no cars and very few visitors.

I hadn't noticed the man pull in; going by his baseball cap, which was adorned with pins and metals, I could tell he was a veteran. It was early in the morning and we were the only two people there. (Well, really there were hundreds of people there, but we were the only ones who were upright.)

I watched as he stood there, cleaning one of the gravestones. It bore a photo of a woman embossed in the marble.

"Is that your wife?" I heard myself asking him. *Laura! What is your problem?* I thought furiously. *Don't get so personal!*

"What was her name?" I hoped he might recognize my level of experience with the subject.

"Dolores," he replied, clearing his voice. "Her name was Dolores."

"May I say hello?" *Are you seriously going to walk over and introduce yourself to a headstone? You are truly weird.*

"Who are you talking to?" my mother asked. We had been on the cell phone together. "I thought you were in the graveyard?"

I put her on speaker phone and held it out to the man. "This is my Mom," I offered as introduction.

"Hi, Mom," he laughed. "My name is Wily."

"Hi, Wily," she replied.

"And I'm Laura," I added, extending my hand to shake his.

We all chatted for a minute, both my Mom and I thanking him for his service to the country.

That's when I was introduced to Dolores.

"Hi, Dolores," I greeted the headstone. "How are you?" *What are you, the grave whisperer now?*

Wily laughed at my polite greeting, and I asked him to tell me a bit about her. "She was a beautiful woman," I added, motioning toward the photograph. She really was; her face was kind, with big brown eyes and a pretty smile. She looked like a good mother, the kind to have her kids' annual portraits taken at Sears.

Geez, Laura. Why not just make the man break down?

And indeed, as Wily stood there, tears started building in his eyes.

"I miss her so much," he choked, the way you would expect a tough, tattooed war veteran to admit defeat. "She was the love of my life. I took one look at her and asked her to dance and that was it. We got married a few months later and never left each other's sides for fifty-six years."

Now I was crying, listening to this old man talk about his life. Born and raised in Yonkers. Korean War vet. Worked in the old carpet mill factory. Raised three children. Has four grandchildren and three great grandchildren. Then came her breast cancer. He took care of her for almost a year. Lives alone now—well, has two cats. Sees the kids regularly. Misses her constantly.

I looked at the headstone to see how long it had been; she had died the day after Mark.

Do I tell him?

No, I thought, tuning back into the conversation. This was not about me. I was here to learn from him and to give him an opportunity to talk about his wife. This is something we don't get to do often—talk about our lost loved ones. People tend worry when you do, thinking you're stuck in grief.

"She was a good woman and I miss her every day, but you gotta live in the present," Wily was saying. "You gotta move on. You can't live in the past," he repeated, wiping his eyes with a real handkerchief, the plaid cotton kind that Dolores probably ironed for him.

We stood there for a few more minutes, now comfortably silent, as we stared at her photo.

"Do you think she sees us?" I asked.

"I hope so," he replied, looking a little wistful. "That's why I come here every single day. They shovel a path just for me in the winter. I come here to tell her I love her, every day."

Maybe that's what fifty-six years of marriage does to a person.

My decision not to bury Mark-in-a-Box at the cemetery wasn't an easy one. Some appreciated the sense of humor and adventure shown in sprinkling him. Others did not. Too bad for them. My only care was that he didn't die in vain.

If nothing else, the sprinklings saved me from a duty like Wily's. There was no need for me to visit a cemetery, feeling impossibly guilty if I missed a day. And how many visits would be enough? Everyday? Once a week? Only on holidays? The 25th of every month? Would the girls and I end up fighting about how they need to go see their father more, like we do about walking the dog or doing chores?

I decided it was much better to have what's left of his ashes in his box on the bookshelf. That way, if I ever needed to, I could do spontaneous things like sprinkle a little sprinkle next to Dolores' plot, as I did the next day.

But while I felt satisfied that I had done the right thing by Mark, something inside of me was still feeling unsettled. Or perhaps unfinished? I can't explain it—things just weren't "there" yet. Even all those miles later, the vortex still raged.

34

The Moment of
Truth

"Aye, Compulsion. How is it that thou meets
with thy friend Death? The monologue went
on. Apparently I represented that which is a
source of her madness in making the ultimate
decision."

—Excerpted from Mark's journals

The ultimate decision to move became instantly clear—there was no way I could continue to live in our house without him.

Everyone always says not to make any big decisions during that first year after losing someone. That includes selling your house and moving your family, I suppose. Okay, fine; I see their point. I'm sure some people create wild fantasies of living on a houseboat in India or becoming an English teacher in Spain, and perhaps you would want to discourage them from acting on impulse without thinking things through.

That's how bereaved minds sometimes work, after all. They look for escape; Greyhound Therapy. But I know all too well how fast your baggage can sneak up on you. You'll sit down on the side of the most beautiful mountain on the most perfect of days and still feel like you're going to suffocate to death right then and there.

And so, I tried to clear some of the daily reminders in The Mark Pittman Hall of Fame. (At least that way, I would stop smelling the underarms of his suits, or would at least have to drive to the local Goodwill to do so.)

Ask anyone and they will tell you the same thing: cleaning out your dead person's closet and removing other personal items is one of the hardest things you can possibly do. You'll suddenly find that you can't part with anything as you put a used tissue atop the "Keep Forever" pile while the "Donate" and "Decide Later" boxes sit empty.

Would it be too macabre to have an upholsterer make ottomans out of his giant leather jackets? And what to do with his collection of music? We counted 1,739 vinyl albums; should I sell them? Keep them? Give them away? (They ended up as wallpaper in Susannah's bedroom.)

What about the musty boxes containing every single story he had ever written, dating back to his time as editor of the high school newspaper? Would the girls ever read them? Should I archive them in acetone paper for eternity? Maybe the mausoleum would like to cover the walls in the basement of urns. I sat reading and categorizing every one of them with the intention of turning them into books for the girls (which I never did).

It went like that for several months. Sorting. Deciding. Crying. Every single thing had to be analyzed in terms of what it meant, how much it meant, did it have a good memory, a story behind it, would the girls want it later, would I want it later, who would want it later, and always, always—when *was* later?

It felt like I was not only erasing him from our lives but invading his privacy in the process. What if I found something personal, a picture or a letter or some papers he never intended me to see? His work files, as well as his divorce papers, were sitting there in clearly marked boxes, but I had never looked at them before and would not do so now. Just because somebody dies doesn't give you the right to go through *all* of their things.

Each decision felt so final—almost like saying goodbye all over again. And the guilt? It was overwhelming. I guess that's what led me to throw away all twenty-two of my own photo albums from growing up, except the ones that started with us. If his memories were gone, I decided, then I would get rid of mine, too.

"I *had* to, Mom," I cried. At this point we were talking on the phone every day. "It would be like having a fire rip through the house and only destroy his things; it wouldn't be right." She understood but told me I would live to regret it. So far, I haven't, and I doubt I ever will.

I stumbled into the deli for coffee the morning of the first big purge.

"And how is your life?" Deli Man asked, looking at me over his drugstore reading glasses.

"It's okay. How is *your* life?"

We both laughed; I tried to parrot his accent (and I did it quite well, I may add). We went outside to smoke, only I was observing, not partaking. (Yes; I was being a good Girl Scout).

"No, but really," he insisted, leaning against the building and taking a big drag. "How are you?"

"Good, I guess. I've been doing a major clean out."

"Yes, I see." He nodded to the smears of Benjamin Moore paint on my jeans. I was a veritable rainbow of house paint shades with lovely poetic names. Wedgewood Blue. Valley View. Sunflower Fields. Purple Passion. White Opulence.

"It's good for you," he continued. "It can be hard, but materials clutter the mind. When you clear, you sometimes find things you never knew you were looking for."

His perception blew me away especially later that day, when I discovered the wooden cigar boxes in Mark's bottom desk drawer.

That's when I knew for certain that Mark knew he was going to die.

He had set up little boxes of memorabilia and trinkets for each of his girls. Without seeing the sonogram photo, it was obvious which belonged to Nell by the marbles and the ticket stub to "Beauty and the Beast," among other things.

Susannah's was easy to figure out too. It included a lock of her hair and a drawing she made for him on Father's Day. Maggie's was attached to the golf club he used to chase the monster out from under her bed. Mine held a private, passionate love letter and poem he had once written for me.

It hit me the minute I found those boxes. Did this mean that Mark had lived like I did, thinking every day would be his last? That he might go down to the basement for a paperclip and never come back? That he would go to sleep and never wake up? Or fall over dead in the park behind the swing as the girls delighted, "Higher, Daddy! Higher!"

I began going through his medical files, looking for anything that would help me to understand. Maybe there'd be a letter from his doctor or a test result—something he hadn't told me.

Easy, Laura. Conscious breathing, remember? Is your breathing relaxed, rhythmic, silent and deep? Now extend the exhale...that's it. It will be okay. You will get through it. Just breathe.

35

Super Susannah
Swims

"'Papa, I can swim,' she called out as the
white-capped rapids hit her shoulders. She
grabbed for his hand, scurrying to the safety
of his arms as quickly as the waters churned.
It was close, but she was safe. Lord, thank
you for not taking another one."

—Excerpted from Mark's journals

When Susannah "announced" that she wanted to swim 3.2 miles across the Hudson River for a leukemia fundraiser, I was surprised...and impressed. Not only did she wish to make a difference in the world, but it was on our wedding anniversary—September 12—and she apparently wanted to mark it in a big way.

The girls had grown up swimming and boating on the Hudson; the water was like their second home. Susannah had also been on a year-round swim team and had qualified for the Junior Olympics in breaststroke.

Her swim coach encouraged her to go for it. Beyond the intense open water training that would be required to safely swim the Hudson, she also needed to raise $650. She did everything on her own through a letter writing campaign, social media outreach, bake sales, and babysitting. I was so proud, I found myself joining the other rah-rah cheer squads of mothers on Facebook.

(And, when one of those Facebook mothers didn't donate to Susannah, after I had bought six boxes of Girl Scout cookies from *her* daughter? Well, I just happened to be passing by her house one day when I scooped a handful of ashes into an old Dunkin' Donuts cup and accidentally threw it onto her perfectly manicured lawn, my middle finger wagging triumphantly in the air. There, balance had been restored to the universe.)

Even with all the professional assurances and money in place, I decided to swim alongside her, to protect her if she needed protecting.

"Mom, no offense, but you swim like a drowning moth." Susannah's evaluation was unapologetic. She was right. But that just meant I was now more determined to do it.

The day arrived. A tiny pinch of Mark inside our swim caps for moral support couldn't hurt, I thought, as Susannah and I lined up with the other participants waiting for the horn to sound. (Who knew amateur swimmers could be so *muscular?*)

On your Mark! Get set! Go! Susannah was in.

And I...wasn't.

"Come on, Mom. You can do it. Jump!" she called, smiling up at me from the water.

"Ready, Mark?" I whispered. "Let's go."

It was an exhilarating, yet terrifying moment of triumph. I took swimming lessons to prepare, but the local Y was very different than the mighty Hudson.

"I can't paddle with you hanging on like that," my kayak guide called out to me. That's the person who paddles next to you...just in case. I made sure mine had lifeguard training, too. Lots of it!

"It'll only be for a minute," I gasped.

"You have to let go," Eileen said. "Just swim; I've got you."

"I can't."

"You have to!"

After being out there for about 40 minutes, the perfectly calm water started churning, which totally freaked me out. Chuck, who was Susannah's guide, took little notice. He just kept merrily paddling his kayak, Susannah swimming alongside of him. Meanwhile, I clutched onto Eileen's kayak like a water bug and this time, I told her, I was not letting go.

"You can do this, Mom," Susannah called back to me, arms slapping at the water.

Her determination was inspiring. If she could keep fighting to move forward, then I had to do the same. *Just. Keep. Swimming.*

Then again...success is all in one's perspective, I guess.

We had gone an impressive 2.1 miles, according to the captain of the "call-it-quits boat," which now had ten people aboard.

"Just take my hand," I called out after finally catching up to her and finding that not only were her lips blue, but that she was shivering through her wetsuit. "We're done here. It's not worth it," I told her.

"I've got this, Mom," she insisted. Just then, a white cap smashed her in the face. The timing couldn't have been better. Now there were twelve people in the boat.

The captain gave us blankets and offered to drop us off close to the finish, so we could swim in to receive our fanfare. Susannah declined, instead vowing to try again next year. Like father, like daughter; and now, like the Good Girl Scout mother.

36

Viking Funeral

"It was a pyre. Rain-soaked ashes and half-
burnt kindling, he waded in to reach the
body, charred and blistered. Thunder cracked,
but a new cry filled the clearing. Samuel
knew that rain does not taste salty."

—Excerpted from Mark's journals

A month after the swim, we were once again at the Hudson as I gently placed a naked Barbie doll on a white handkerchief in one of Mark's cigar boxes. We were coming up on the first anniversary of his death, and a memorial service at our somewhat dilapidated boat club felt in order.

Mark always said what he really wanted was a Viking funeral—to go out on a burning raft—though I'm not sure he knew I would take him seriously, the same way Hunter Thompson's friends did when complying with his wish to be fired out of a cannon.

He had dressed up as a Viking for Halloween that year. I wonder if this is why.

I also wondered if Mark knew that, in the Viking tradition, the barbarians sent a naked virgin out on the burning boat. Oh, well; I was pretty sure Nell's Barbie doll wouldn't mind being sacrificed. And that Mark would certainly love a last cigar.

"The biggest one you have, not the skinny ones with plastic tips on them," I told Deli Man. "Do you have any from Cuba? Aren't those the best?"

"You really shouldn't smoke cigars," he told me, concerned. "You are better smoking eighty cigarettes than one cigar."

This made me laugh. "No, no. It's not for me, Deli Man."

"Something special, I see," he said, nodding sagely. "That's why you are nervous about this very important cigar." He handed me one from the humidor, not the metal rack. "Go do whatever it is that you're doing. Good luck. You can pay me later. Next time you come."

And so, a gathering of about eighty friends sent Mark out on a burning raft into the Hudson. His vessel bore gifts: piles of BBQ ribs; poker cards; a signed Yankees cap; a bottle of really good champagne; farewell letters; books; cards; photos—whatever offerings people wanted to send him off with. Then, once we had set it on fire and out onto the river (guided by a few of his closest comrades), everyone threw a single sunflower into the Hudson.

The memorial service provided just the right blend of poignancy and humor to do him justice. All the same, it didn't feel right to send him out like that without offering the earth something in return.

"A crabapple tree? Do you really think that's an appropriate choice?" I asked my friend Kate, a garden designer, while trying not to sound offended that anyone would suggest planting a *crabapple* tree in someone's honor. She explained why—it's one of the few trees that has the potential to survive on a wind-whipped river like the Hudson.

And so we dug.

Then it was back to the house for a backyard bonfire and giant pots of chili. Dear and loving friends, warm food, a lot of laughter—the only thing missing was Mark.

Until the Bad Girl Scout had an idea.

That was my first time sprinkling his ashes into food. And it was only the tiniest bit, like the turn of a pepper grinder, more symbolic than anything...but be forewarned. Eat at the Pittmans' and you never know—you just might eat a Pittman.

37

Thanks-Taking

"The plan was to have no plan. No give and take. That way, there was nothing to look forward to or to look back upon with missing regret."

—Excerpted from Mark's journals

Being amongst friends made his first "deathiversary" bearable, but really the only place I really wanted to be was back at bereavement group.

Despite never having been a joiner, it helped to be with people who also lay awake at night with visions of coffins dancing in their heads. Forget the sugar plums and fairies. Who would put up the tree or light the menorah? What about presents? Should we let our kids buy a present for their dead loved ones if it makes them feel better, or is that truly an exercise in denial?

Poor Yolanda worried over who would carve the turkey now that her life partner was dead of brain cancer at only forty-seven years old. We spent an entire session talking about it. It might seem ridiculous to focus on—this giant question of "Who Will Carve Yolanda's Turkey"—but it was a giant deal to her, and now to us.

And that's the thing—as tedious as it was, we all *got it*. We understood that she was keeping Bryan alive by bringing him into the holiday fracas. It wasn't a "real" problem, but it *was* a coping mechanism.

We encouraged Yolanda to let it go—to stop worrying—and just let whoever it might be step up to the carving board. It would all work out, we promised. But advice is always easier to give than to take. No one truly understands how another person feels unless it happens to them; and even then, everyone's experience is different.

One of the hardest things about losing a loved one is that a major part of you dies with them, yet you are expected to carry on as though you are still a whole person.

That's why people shouldn't say things like, "He's in a better place now." *Oh, you've been there? Tell me, what does his new house look like?*

"You're young. You'll find love again." *So, what you're saying is, my husband can be easily replaced? Apparently, you did not know the man.*

"I know just how you feel…" *Really? I don't even know how I feel.*

The closer we got to THE DAY, the more I wanted to run. I had cleaned the house and was all set to make Mark's favorite—apple and sausage stuffing. But then the wave of dread would set in—the one with the power to change plans.

So, how about Thanksgiving in Florida, girls? Sanibel Island? We'd do a house swap; all I have to pay for was airfare. And thanks to frequent flier miles earned from putting everything—even groceries—on my AMEX card, I only had to buy one ticket (a steal at $225).

Now, we had a *new* Thanksgiving plan.

38

Ashes and Apples and Gators, Oh My!

"He paused on the river bank for a moment
before striking. I put a single shot between
his eyes. It was either that or be killed
right there, out in the open."

—Excerpted from Mark's journals

We boarded the plane at LaGuardia Airport, where I sprinkled Mark in first class when no one rich was looking.

A short flight ensued—without panic, thank you very much—though Susannah began complaining that her ears hurt as soon as the plane began its landing.

Like any good mother, I had gum in my purse. "It happens to everyone," I told her.

Once we arrived at the beach house, I gave her two Tylenol and tucked her into bed, worried she'd caught a cold.

At 1 am, she came into my room, whimpering.

"Do you want to go to the hospital?" I asked, completely expecting her to say no. That's how Moms know when a child is truly sick—when they say yes, take me to the hospital.

When she asked if Daddy could come with us, I felt like the worst mother in the world.

She held his box in her little lap, tears of pain shooting out of her eyes.

The diagnosis? Two bleeding, ruptured eardrums. The doctor on duty gave her a prescription for codeine, a get-out-of-marine-biology-camp note, and a plastic vomit bag for the car ride back to the house. She used all three.

She wasn't allowed to go under water but going to the beach itself was okay—especially the one with all the sand dollars.

"Don't worry, Susannah, I promise you won't get water in your ears," I reassured her. "The water's only up to your chest. Just wear these," handing her earplugs.

Catching sand dollars is easy. You just feel along the bottom of the ocean floor with your feet and do a marsupial-like grab with your toes, then reach down to pluck them, one at a time. It seemed like a fun way to spend the day, but she wasn't enjoying herself, even though she had stopped throwing up.

"What's wrong with your sister?" I asked Nell after she and her cousin returned from the camp Susannah was forced to miss out on. "Why is she crying? She said the pain medication was working really well."

"Maybe because her father died," Nell said in her witty way.

"I heard that!" shouted Susannah. "And I am *not* crying because Daddy died. It's *mean*, Mom."

"What's mean, Susannah?" I really didn't understand.

"Killing all those poor little sand dollars!" She was now holding one upside down to show me how it was gasping for air before shooting me a murderous look like I had just clubbed a baby seal to death.

I explained that the sand dollar was okay. "It's not gasping for air. They breathe through their feet, not through those moving parts."

"It's still mean to kill them," she insisted. "They're living beings too, you know."

I tried to reason with her. "You didn't get upset when you caught that huge catfish last summer off Gramma's dock, Susannah."

"That's different, Mom. We put it back."

She had a point.

"She should start a nonprofit called 'Susannah Saves the Sand Dollars,'" her cousin joked. I thought Susannah would see the humor, but no luck; nothing's funny when your eardrums are bleeding, I guess.

You're also not likely to find it funny when your grandmother—unknowingly—makes a table decoration out of, what else? Sand dollars.

Thanksgiving that year was a little unconventional, and not just in terms of the location. There was no turkey or pecan pie; instead, we made spaghetti and meatballs and took turns with a hammer, smashing coconuts for dessert.

We did have a special dinner guest, however.

One minute we were sitting there, and the next we saw it lazing out of the canal, one gross claw at a time, until it pulled its belly onto the grass.

That's when Mr. Alligator spotted us—three tasty morsels of human flesh sunbathing in bikinis by the pool. It wasn't necessarily licking its chops at this point, but I wasn't interested in waiting to find out what its next move would be, either.

Not knowing whether alligators were like dogs who loved a good chase before biting the back of your leg off, we had to think quickly.

"Dip the apple in Daddy's ashes and throw him the apple, Mom," Nell instructed. "It will distract him. Then we'll slowly back away into the house, and if it comes after us, I'll thrown the lawn chair at it."

"Run!" we screamed when the apple pegged him in the forehead. Safely behind the sliding glass door, we could now watch the gator eat his kill—candied Mark!

39

I'm Dreaming of a Mark Christmas

"My dreams aren't much babe, but they're all
I've got left."

—Excerpted from Mark's journals

Winter set in, as it usually does. Snow covers the ground and pretty soon, it's holiday time again.

The girls and I did our best; we put up our first fake Christmas tree ever (it fell down); I got them a puppy, who they named Clyde (it peed on their beds); I lit the fireplace (smoke backed up into the house).

And sure, I *could* have called a neighbor to check the flue, but to me, asking for help would have been like admitting I was incapable of managing my life, smoke-filled house or not. Then I would fill with self-doubt, which would make me feel out of control, and then I would weaken. And then what? What would happen to the girls if something happened to me? I *had* to be strong. I had to keep my job, build fires, ward off alligators, plan Christmas, keep it all together.

Part of feeling sorry for myself could perhaps be blamed on the hormones marinating my brain. Yes, because I now had yet another thing to manage—menopause. To think, I might not have noticed the gray hairs either. Thankfully, the hairdresser was kind enough to point them out. Of course, I had to put on my new reading glasses to see them, because, you know, my eyes were going, too.

Still, I got the best present I could ever ask for that Christmas—a dream about Mark.

We were falling down laughing at ourselves for being so happy to see each other while kissing in a field of sunflowers...until he floated up and away from me, off into the sky, like a deflating balloon bearing away his incredible smile and I-love-you eyes.

I awoke wrapped in a blanket of him. It felt as if he were right there next to me, alive again. Then, almost immediately, after realizing it had been a dream, out came a grief burst—one of those sudden, shuddering eruptions of intense, wild woman crying. These bursts are different than regular crying; they can end as quickly as they begin, like tropical rain showers that erupt and hang in the air until the sun breaks in through the humid haze.

Too bad the sun hadn't even begun to think of rising yet as the tears pounded down on my pillow. Or was it his pillow? I felt like Alice in Wonderland, falling down the sleepy rabbit hole into a giant unknown world.

"Girls, I know it's Christmas Day, but do you want to go skiing?" I asked, as if I had planned it as a present. But really, I had just thought of it.

40

Goodwill Hunting

"Her progress was slow. It was painstaking to watch her deliberation, like a slow-moving hell on earth for which she suffered every time she thought of him."

—Excerpted from Mark's journals

By spring, we had more than passed the "Don't make any big decisions in the first year" marker that everyone talks about. It was time to consider leaving our home and all its memories behind and finding some place to start...if not new, then at least over again. And, while it was only a mile down the road, the house I found for sale on Realtor.com was perfect—the smallest and ugliest on the street, which also meant the cheapest.

I'd even found a familiar face at the town's deli when I walked in for a Diet Snapple.

"DELI MAN! What are you doing here?"

"I work here! Where have you been? I have not seen you! What are you doing here?"

"I live here," I said. "Well, almost live here."

It was actually Deli Man who helped me make the final decision to move. I told him about the house: that it was less than half the price of the average home in Hastings-on-Hudson, a cute little village of 9,000, as opposed to the 200,000 in the city of Yonkers. Sure, you get what you pay for—it was being sold "as is," which is code for "it needs a ton of work," but it had potential. Most importantly, the kids could walk to school, and they already had friends there, which would make for an easy transition.

Was it fate or folly that led me to sign the papers that day?

My mother gently proposed that I replace our marital bed—to start fresh in the "new" house without it. "You can't hold onto Mark forever, honey," she said. "I know it's hard, but you have to move forward."

"But it's our bed," I protested, "and it's certified by astronauts as being the most comfortable on earth! And why rid of the sheets? We picked them out together."

It wasn't like I lit candles in my bedroom or held Ouija Board pajama parties to summon Mark from the spirit world. I just liked our bedding.

Letting go of the material past, I soon learned, doesn't miraculously make the present more bearable. Moving meant truly saying goodbye to our memories. Mark carrying Susannah into the house at one week old; playing dolls with the girls in the tree house that he built; cutting firewood in the yard; getting blown off the table when he forgot to turn off the breaker before installing the new chandelier.

I guess I hadn't made as much progress on the path to enlightenment as I thought. Part of that process is letting go of the emotional and spiritual past. But that was alright. The universe saw fit to give me another chance when my father died.

Robert. Lung cancer. Lucky Strikes. Age 84.

My father and I had had no Hallmark moments in between—not even on his deathbed. Twice I put flights on hold, and twice I cancelled them for fear of seeing him die.

The group understood my decision. I guess I went back for that kind of support, to relieve me of my guilt. We grievers have a tremendous capacity for being non-judgmental.

I was happy, however, to have something to remind me of my father. My brother had mailed it to me: Robert's giant Grizzly bear rug. While I am against hunting purely for sport, it was already too late for poor "Teddy." I had a special affection for that bear, maybe because I felt so sorry for it, the same as I still do for my father.

41
Seriously? Dating?

"I now live in self-imposed celibacy, a hood over my head and my eyes downcast. Stripped of part of my humanity, I have gained a little of the androgyny of God."

—Excerpted from Mark's journals

At bereavement group, we had moved onto the topic of...dating. It was the last session, and apparently, I was the only one who wasn't or hadn't been, but this is not what astonished me. What astonished me was that everyone was sitting there week after week, talking about how to cope with wills and bills and clothes and cars and messed-up families and deep feelings and lost love, all while managing kids and homework and housework and everything else... and they were somehow *dating* on top of all that?

"Are you freaking kidding me?" I wanted to shout. I was stunned; some group members were only a few months widowed. They seemed equally surprised that someone with more than two years under her belt had yet to, well, *remove* her belt.

I immediately called my friend Connie.

"You are *not* going to believe this," I told her. "People at bereavement group are dating!"

"I'll be right over!" she said, not realizing she had an agenda—*mine*!

While waiting, I decided to ask Google what *it* thought: "When does the average widow start dating again?"

The articles talked about how the loss of a loved one is "a source of intense emotional stress." *Blah, blah.* Experts said we have to "express" and "deal with" our feelings of loss before we can reorganize our lives. *Duh!* One reported that "normal grief" often follows a fairly predictable pattern, and that by the end of the first year, survivors often become "more active socially, get out more, see people, resume their interests," and, yes, start dating. *Oh dear!*

Connie showed up less than thirty minutes later—record time, for her—with a bottle of wine in hand, bless her soul.

"They're all sitting there, talking about dating, and I'm not even remotely thinking about it. And my dead person has been dead for a lot longer than a lot of their dead people have been dead," I complained. "According to these articles, I'm already more than a year behind schedule!"

I could tell she wasn't listening. She was clicking away on her laptop instead.

"Well, maybe it's about time, Bunny Bun Bun 007," she said.

"Who's Bunny Bun Bun 007?"

"It's you," she announced. "Or rather, your password."

"For what?" I still wasn't following.

"Match.com."

I was simultaneously horrified and intrigued.

"You seriously just put me on Match.com?"

"Yup and you're gonna like it. Do you want to look like this for the rest of your life?" Connie asked, pulling up a photo of an old craggy-faced lady dressed in black mourning clothes. "Or this?" This time it was a picture of me in a t-shirt and cut-off jeans on the bow of our boat. "The choice is yours."

Maybe she was right. Maybe everyone in bereavement group was right. Maybe holding onto the past was not the best coping mechanism for truly "moving on" or "getting over it."

I had always imagined online dating to be the digital equivalent of trawling strip mall singles bars on the Island of Misfit Toys. But some of these guys didn't look so bad. And hey, if the bereavement people were doing it, maybe I should, too!

Google reported 54,250,000 single adults in the United States that year, with a full 41,250,000 of them having signed up on at least one of the 2,500 dating sites out there. Just over half of all users (53.4 percent) were men, though it bears remembering that ten percent of sex offenders report using online dating to meet people.

But even adjusting for total creeps, it seemed my chances were decent—from a statistical point of view. According to what I read, men's preferences broke down to 42 percent liking the Modern Career Girl type, 34 percent liking the Girl Next Door, and 24 percent going for the Hottie.

"But I'm not a hottie!" I cried. "I'm also not a big career type and the girl next door doesn't smoke cigarettes with a deli man."

"Stop stalling!" Connie said.

"Okay. Alright, do it!" I winced as she uploaded the boat photo and wrote whatever it is she wrote in my online profile.

Several days later, Mariano—to whom I quickly assigned the name MmmMariano, as in MmmMmm-Good—appeared in my emails. He was six years younger than me, but otherwise we matched on a lot of points. He went to a great school and owned his own business, and as a bonus, he was tall, really handsome, and had a nice smile.

Coffee? Sure, I thought, why not?

I wasn't nervous; neither did it feel like I was cheating on Mark. I was looking forward to meeting someone who knew nothing about me, or us. Maybe I could be the old me, the fun me, not the "bereaved

widow who still sometimes slept with her husband's ashes at night"
me.

A few days later, we went to lunch, and then dinner a few nights
after that—on a Friday, which (according to Connie), indicated that
MmmMariano was seriously interested.

But instead of returning his kiss goodnight, I pulled away.

"I'm sorry," I said, standing there feeling like a complete idiot.

"It's okay," he reassured me. "I really like you, and I want to get
to you know you and date you, but I understand. You're not ready.
You need time."

"I do." I liked him, too. "Just not now. Not yet. Can I call you?"

The tears that flowed later as I lay awake in bed were not for him
or even for Mark.

Part IV:
The Second
Trip: Double
the Love

42

Setting Our Sights

"Sunday mornings often started by squinting
at a clear blue sky. I rolled the sleeping
bag back up and put on my shades to face the
breaking sun. It was a little warmer here,
but not much. The chill covered my thighs
with goosebumps as I slid back into my jeans.
I headed east to hit the main road."

—Excerpted from Mark's journals

Before considering any of love's lofty requirements, I needed to set a slightly more achievable goal: another trip. Because I was still not settled. We needed more time together. I needed to further free him from his box, to see him living again so that maybe I could, too.

Mark's new life, nor mine, would not be complete without a part of him resting among the red-rock buttes, steep canyon walls, and pine forests in Sedona. Or at the Grand Canyon or the Carlsbad Canyons. The art scene in Santa Fe would also have been top on his list. The Mojave Desert. Denver. These were the places he still needed to be.

And no, obviously it wasn't the smartest thing to do—to take off again, especially just before mortgaging a house—but it was now or never. Plus, a friend from work would go on part of the trip with us.

He was a former cop, which meant he would keep us safe...and he could read a map.

Now all I needed to do was come up with the money. According to my calculations, gas for HaRVey would cost $920 if we drove 6,000 miles at $2.50 per gallon. Add food and fun on top of that for, say, one month, meant I'd have to come up with about $1,500, or $50 a day. It was more than I had, but I could easily sell some of our furniture (which I didn't want now, anyway) and that nice Ethan Allen rug. Plus, one of the office interns was now renting our attic bedroom for $500 a month. Add it all up, and I could pretty much make it happen.

Since the head rarely follows the heart, I made my decision based on Susannah. She had entered and won a Mother's Day essay writing contest for the New York Post. When I read it in the Sunday paper, I knew we had more sprinkling to do.

"When my dad died, my mom was really, really sad, but she is almost a better mom now because it's like she has to double-love us. She is a lot of fun, and our friends say they wish she was their mom. She always says she wants to be a kid when she grows up. Last summer, my mom, sister, and I drove our RV across the country. It was so much fun. My mom is awesome like that. She makes the best of things."

—SUSANNAH PITTMAN, *Yonkers, NY*

The day we were leaving, I stopped by to see Deli Man.

"Guess what, Deli Man!" I called out. He was back in the storeroom, stacking cans of cat food.

"Let me guess. You are going away on vacation again this year."

"How'd you know?"

"Because you know it was good for you and your girls last year and you want to do it again."

He told me to be safe and to make sure to see him when I got back. Then he handed me two packs of pink bubble gum.

"On the house. For your girls," he said, pushing them into my hand. "Goodbye, and good luck my friend."

That same day, right around 2:00 pm, the mailman delivered a package—a black and white photo of Lucille Ball wearing a Superman shirt and a motorcycle helmet, perched on the ledge of a window with a pigeon at her feet. She's not ready to jump, necessarily, but you know she's up to something.

The card read, "Oh Lucy, Lucy, Lucy." It wasn't signed; it didn't have to be.

John had just started up his new law practice and had zero time available for any more misadventures. That's why he sent Lucy—to be my guardian angel.

43

If You Can't Stand the Heat, Drive in the Other Direction

"Looks like we're riding into the big one.
Clouds are massed in the east, lightning
spittle comes in crooked jags. Blue sky at
our backs, dark streaks cascade forward into
the line of wildfire ripping through the
mountains."

—Excerpted from Mark's journals

First stop: Cary, NC to visit my parents and meet up with Robbie, who was there on business anyway.

The girls and I had time for plenty of sprinkles on the way there. There was Newark, New Jersey—the Smelliest Place on Earth—where we each grabbed a handful and threw him out the RV windows on the Turnpike, which he would have particularly appreciated; we ran him up and down the Rocky Balboa steps in Philadelphia, and sprinkled him at Independence Hall, by the Liberty Bell, at the Betsy Ross house, and at the Italian Market, right by the sausages.

He went over the bridge in Delaware before leaving him at John Hopkins University in Baltimore, in hopes that they might be able to find a cure for hearts. Then he went to the Basilica of the National Shrine of the Assumption of the Blessed Virgin Mary since it was clear that I would never want to have sex again.

Washington, DC, was an important stop. He got sprinkles at all the museums, memorials, and monuments, before leaving a heaping portion of him at the Federal Reserve Building. The lawsuit was still tangled up in the courts, and I wanted to make sure he could keep an eye on the process.

"BACK DOOR OPEN!" announced my mother's alarm system when we arrived.

I grew to hate that thing. It took its job too seriously, to the point of locking me out a few days later at 7 am when I left the hermetically sealed air-conditioned zone of Subzero, granite, and central vac systems to breathe real air. After banging on my mom's bedroom window for a few minutes, I just couldn't hold it any longer and peed right there in her Zen garden next to the Buddha. Hopefully he didn't mind getting a little wet in the rush of it all.

My mom explained that she had set the security system to its highest level. "There have been a lot of burglaries in the area," she explained. "We need the alarm on at all times."

"Oh, puh-leeze Mom. Really? That's ridiculous. You live in a nice neighborhood; we don't even lock our doors in Yonkers."

That night, someone broke into the RV and stole the kids' iPods. And yes, she said I told you so.

The next morning, Robbie showed up just in time for breakfast. We sat at the kitchen table with egg sandwiches in one hand, an atlas in the other, and the computer on the table.

"This is not looking so good. The southwest is on fire," he reported like a TV news broadcaster as he pointed out the hot spots.

"What do you mean, not looking so good?" I asked, still wearing the pink pajamas my mother-in-law had sent to me for Christmas one year.

"'A vast wildfire, measuring half the size of the state of Rhode Island and described as the worst fire in Arizona history, continues to surge across eastern Arizona,'" he reported, reading from the computer screen and looking a little tense. "Thousands have been evacuated!

"What's more," he continued in that Breaker, Breaker, 1-9 voice, "It's spreading and threatening the entire Southwest!"

Robbie was perhaps overly cautious. John and I would have just driven straight into the fire and figured things out from there.

I called a newsroom in Arizona. It was true; wildfires everywhere. I tried a newsroom in Denver, and then Santa Fe; same thing.

While I didn't necessarily believe all the news hype, there wasn't a lot I could do about it. That's what Robbie was supposed to be there for—to back me up. But now he was backing out. His new plan was to attend a friend's wedding on a goat farm in Cape Breton, Nova Scotia.

I started cursing. (It helps to swear when I'm mad; the F-bomb especially seems to act as a natural Xanax. It makes me feel so much better, and so quickly, too.)

Robbie just looked at me and smiled.

"What's so funny?" I demanded.

"You."

That really upset me. We had an objective here, and it wasn't to be a wedding planner on some stupid goat farm. We had ashes to spread!

The trips were more than just "getting away from it all" or having a "nice little change of pace." They bonded us in grief and empowered us to live as independent, strong women who could survive anything.

So having Robbie treat the whole thing like a weekend excursion? *Forget* that.

After going upstairs to change into some real clothes and figure out what to do next, my mom confronted me.

"Honey," she said in that heavy doom-and-gloom tone, the one she only broke out for dramatic announcements, "George and Wendy and I are worried about you."

"Really, Mom? And why is that?" I was being really rude to my own mother, but I also doubted that George and Wendy had ever had this conversation with her, and I hated it when she cornered me.

"We think you are grieving...too hard," she said.

"What is that supposed to mean, grieving...too hard? Should I grieve softly, then? Because the last time I checked, *your* husband was standing upright. In fact, he's downstairs drinking coffee as we speak! Mine's dead. He'll never have a cup of coffee again—unless I give him an eyedropper full in his box. So sorry, but I'm going to have to grieve however it comes out of me."

She stood there looking at me as I whipped my shoes across the room, telling her to try walking in them. Then she rocked me as I cried.

I'm not sure how long she held me, but I know it was a long time, because when lunch was being served, I was still wearing the pink pajamas.

44

On the Road Again

"I lean against the gas pump, debating whether
we can get out of here without paying for
it. We could make a run for it, but then we'd
only catch ourselves."

—Excerpted from Mark's journals

The girls and I decided to do our own thing and catch up with Robbie on the Canadian border. Our first stop? Busch Gardens in Williamsburg, Virginia for a little rock 'n roller coaster action. If we weren't going to hike mountains, at least we could fly through the sky.

We sprinkled on, heading to Newport, Rhode Island for a few days on the beach. The girls had never been boogie boarding before. And sure, they weren't coasting on ten-foot breakers, but it was still a great new experience for them. This is what these trips are about; replacing our emotions with experiences to build new foundations or at least fill in some of the empty holes by letting nothing hold us back.

We were now sprinkling in a place that Mark and I had been together. It was there that my non-seafood eaters agreed to try whole boiled lobster for the first time. Only, it tasted like rubber bands marinated in sewer water. How can a lobster restaurant ruin lobster?

Annoyed by the high bill for uneaten food, I lied to the parking lot attendant in an attempt to at least recoup the $20 parking fee.

"Oh, my husband must have paid it, but he's not here in the RV right now," I told the cashier in the booth. A double lie—he was right there in the front seat, chillin' in his box.

"There's supposed to be a pass in the window," she said, admiring her long pink fingernails. "I don't see one there."

"Neither do I," I told her, pretending to look for the pass. "Who knows where he put it!"

"Men," she snarled.

"Yeah, men," I griped back, playing on her sympathies. "Can't live with 'em, can't live without 'em."

"Hey, I'm in here and I resent that," Mark would have called from his box if he could speak. But then, if he could we wouldn't be in this parking lot, now, would we?

The girls just sat there, afraid to say anything and afraid not to say anything, looking as though they had swallowed butterflies. But the "nice" parking lot attendant lady said not to worry, that she had an ex-husband who was useless too. She understood exactly what I was going through with mine.

She stubbed out her cigarette on the ground in disgust, as if the Marlboro was really a man.

Mark would have done the right thing, for sure, but I didn't feel like earning my Girl Scout honesty badge that day.

Go away, I mentally shushed him. *You know how much I love lobster and how bad it must have been for me not to eat it.*

He actually wouldn't have said anything back in real life. He never did; he would just sit there quietly, waiting for me to work things out for myself, all the while wearing that amused smile on his face as he watched my little brain go into overdrive.

Damn him!

"Umm...excuse me," I said to the lady. "I have a confession to make. I...umm...I'm sorry, I just totally lied to you. I didn't pay;

neither did my husband. In fact, he's dead—that's how much I just lied. See, he's right here in this box of ashes."

She looked in the window, glancing at the ashes without a change in expression. It was clear that she had seen a lot of long, cold winters. Or hey, maybe one of her husbands lived in a box, too. She looked back up at me.

"You're a good mom. You just taught your girls a valuable lesson. Never lie, girls. And when you do, 'fess up immediately."

A five-dollar tip and twenty bucks later, we were on our way.

We were glad to have time to ourselves...*without* Robbie... the vacation wrecker. The girls and I ended up renting the same adorable private beach cottage at the Castle Hill Inn where Mark and I had spent a romantic weekend just before our wedding. It was a giant splurge, but when the girls remembered seeing the pictures in our photo album, how could I not?

It was so cool to be able to sprinkle Mark at the exact site of our "From Here to Eternity" scene, where we made out against the boulder in the water. I sat there counting how many times we'd likely kissed over fifteen years, coming up with 27, 379 times or about five a day, with some of the most memorable being right there.

Still, things aren't always Facebook perfect. Mark and I had argued about whether to go out to dinner or order room service that weekend, and now the girls began arguing over who'd spotted a particular seashell first.

"Can we have some quiet here?" I snapped, mid-sprinkle. "Your father and I are having a moment."

It's funny how the scattering of ashes had become so familiar that the act could now occupy the same moment as petty bickering. That's not to say the ceremonies had become routine or meaningless; it's that I realized they had simply become a part of who we are and what we do as a family.

As we waved goodbye to the cottage and drove down Ocean Ave., past all the famous mansions like the Breakers, Chateau-sur-Mer, and others, the girls promised to read all the books in the RV (which included Steinbeck's *Travels with Charley*) if it meant they would become smart enough to make enough money to afford their own castles in Newport.

Funny; they didn't mention anything about getting a mansion by marrying a rich man. Maybe I *was* teaching them a few things, after all.

Now in Massachusetts, we took Mark's ashes to Walden Pond, where he could read and linger in the gardens all day. Shh...we also let him swim with the sharks at the Boston Aquarium; and he's now in the stairwell at the very top of the Bunker Hill monument.

He also got an ample sprinkle in the bushes of an ex-boyfriend on Monument Square for good measure.

45

We Are the People,
the Walmart People

"He stands a few feet away, asking the usual
questions. I think I told him I was a nuclear
engineer on my way to testify at the state
house. Wily tells him he's a drummer in a
punk band on his way to a gig in Fresno."

—Excerpted from Mark's journals

One of the biggest things the trips allowed for was saying, out loud (so that I could get used to hearing the words), "I am widowed," or, "My husband/their father died," or, "He lives up there," while pointing to the sky.

Maybe if I said it enough times, I would start to believe it—and maybe even start to get over it.

And who better to practice on than strangers, especially after a good night's sleep at Walmart, which often welcomes overnight parking to "citizens of the road." (Most casinos, truck stops, and agritourism sites also allow for overnight stays, but you can't beat twenty-four-hour patrols, security cameras, brightly-lit parking lots, and around-the-clock access to America's best junk food.)

The average female warehouse shopper was always a perfect target. Mid-forties, jeans and/or work blouse, but nothing overly stylish or impractical; salt of the earth. Her cart overflowing with everything from groceries to bath towels, she would be wearing a simple wedding band with nice French manicured nails. You could tell she was a busy office worker, juggling life with kids, husbands and dogs. She was the sort of woman you could count on for a favor and to always do the right thing by her family, her friends and her co-workers.

"My husband Mark loved these chocolate chip cookies," I would say, meeting her eyes. "But since he died, and I can't share them with him anymore, I'm going to eat this whole bag by myself. Unless, of course, you'd like one?" I would offer, turning to her.

She would then feel badly and give me her shoulder...and her ear...before asking:

1. "You're so young to be widowed. How old was he?" This is a fear-based question. It means she's worried the same thing could happen to her.
2. "How long were you married?" This meant she wondered how much time she could possibly have left with her husband.
3. "How did he pass?" In other words, did her husband have any symptoms?

This was the question I liked most—the third one—the one I aimed for. Now I could get to the hard part by telling her how I tried to give him CPR, but how it was too late. If she was really curious, I would tell her everything—all the details—so I could get used to hearing, breathing and living them myself.

And always, in the end, I would try to make myself feel better by asking: "At least I was with him, right? Imagine if he died and I didn't know what happened to him, or if I didn't get to tell him how much we loved him. I really hope he heard me. Do you think he did?"

They always said yes which always made me feel better. Then we would talk about how I was spreading his ashes and how I was teaching my girls to be strong...

Often times, the nice ladies would stand there and cry with me. Then they would hug me, and I let them because the truth was, I wanted them to. I needed to rest my head against their hearts and let them stroke my hair and offer me prayers and strong encouragement, to share in the strength they had gained through overcoming their own burdens, whether it be burying their beautiful babies, getting divorced, juggling several jobs, helping their aging parents, or simply being there for a friend going through a hard time.

But in the end, I needed them to tell me it would all be okay; that I was a good wife and a good mom, and that I would survive this and that I did everything I could to save him.

Those women are the nicest in the world. They know the value of things—even dead husbands.

Of course, things didn't always go as planned. Once, while staying in the parking lot of a Walmart in Maine, we had gone in to surf the shelves for our evening's entertainment when I heard a crash. I knew immediately who and where it came from. Susannah!

She had slammed one of the handicap scooters into a stack of cardboard boxes! Now, normally I wouldn't encourage go-karting on handicapped scooters through Walmart (or anywhere else, for that matter), but there *were* seven of them sitting there unused, it *was* past midnight, and the kids *were* restless. To be fair, Susannah had twisted her ankle hiking a few days earlier and *was* having trouble walking so the scooter was fair game.

"Young lady!" an employee's voice called out. Only Nell swiftly outsmarted him by whipping around the corner just in time for Susannah to hop on-board and make their way toward the front doors.

"Where do you girls think you're going? Get back here!" he yelled, porky cheeks flushing as he charged after them.

What else was there to do but pretend I didn't know those bad girls and continue eating cookies with my new friends? There was a group of six of us swapping stories by the register at this point.

"Kids," I remarked to Shelia, the cashier, who had joined the conversation. "No respect."

"You got that right," she scowled, words clipped through bright red lipstick. "Store policy says they can't ride them things, and now *I* gotta clean up the boxes."

I felt bad—really bad—but I wasn't about to go down for anything. I paid for the cookies and scurried out as fast as I could.

Once back in HaRVey, the girls and I broke into one of our road anthems: "Big hair, dreadlocks, little skirt, red box. Hot dog, puppeteer, smiley shorts, swipe right here. We are the people, the Walmart people!"

As we drove along on our grand adventure, someone would inevitably ask what we were doing on the edge of their cornfield town in Anywhere, USA.

"I know: tell them we are homeschooled and Mom's a scientist researching cow poop state by state," Susannah decided.

Nell had a better idea: "We can pretend to be British and say we got lost and ended up in...wait, where are we? Maine? I thought we were in New Hampshire. Okay, so tell them we got lost in Maine on our way to New Hampshire."

We would get a lot of live ones at gas stations, in particular. "Where is your father today, girls?" a woman asked, almost on cue. We were doing our regular drill at the time: Nell was pumping the gas, Susannah was washing windows, and I was stuck checking the tire pressure on all six tires. (RVs have two rear tires on both sides which require the tester to lie on the ground to reach the valve stems. That's why neither girl wanted that job.)

"Oh, he's on a trip. A very long trip," Susannah replied.

"Yeah, in the bathroom," Nell added. "He's been in there for like two years."

"I know what you mean," the lady said. "My husband takes forever, too."

That's the kind of humor that had previously landed Mark in a potted plant at the Burger Queen restaurant in Provincetown and "ashes overboard" while deep sea fishing in Wellfleet. In Bangor, Mark found himself eating ribs and country dancing in a restaurant parking lot.

And, oops! Looks like he somehow ended up getting sprinkled in a guitar case when I thought no one was looking. After all, Mark could play a mean couple of songs on his vintage Fender, so it was worth the risk. How else would he get to tour with a band?

"Excuse me. What are you doing?" I heard a man's voice say.

Busted!

"Oh, uh, can you point me in the direction of the bathroom, please?" I said. There was no way I was looking for a bathroom in the equipment room; that was obvious, as was the dash of gray powder against the black felt case.

He asked me what I had stolen. When I told him nothing, I hadn't taken anything, he seemed to believe me. It wasn't like I could hide a drum set in my pants.

"Then what are you doing in here? This is private property." He didn't look mad, but he also didn't look very happy. Actually, he looked kind of cool, in a, "I'm the frontman in an R&B band" kind of way.

"This is going to sound crazy, but..." I started telling him about Mark and our trip and the tiny bit of ashes I had sprinkled in the guitar case so that Mark could travel with them.

I've seen men cry before, but not on stage, and certainly not the way Ethan James of the Elroys did that night as he sang "When a Man Loves a Woman" in dedication to Mark and me.

"This one goes out to a very special couple on their very special journey," he told the audience as he wiped his eyes with the sleeve of his denim work shirt.

I saw his eyes searching for mine in a crowd of swaying couples. After a few beats, they found me, leaning against a tree, smiling back.

"Thank you," I mouthed.

The next day, it was off to Acadia National Park for a blueberry pie and sprinkle picnic on the rocks.

We were having a good time, riding down the highway, talking and laughing and fighting for space and sandwiches. That is, until HaRVey died.

I don't know much about car engines, but at least I know enough to recognize that the belt that runs the alternator that attaches to the battery (or something like that) had snapped. It looked like a giant rubber band cut in half just dangling there. I quickly closed the hood for fear someone would stop to help... I mean kill us. As I saw it, we only had one option.

"It's only a few more miles," I told the girls as we walked down the road in search of a cell phone tower, gas station or store where we could get help. But inside, I was worried we'd never find one or that someone would break into the RV and steal everything inside. "This is fun! Come on! Let's skip!"

A few calls, a tow truck, a few hours, a few hundred dollars and we were on our way.

Where was Robbie when I needed him? I'll tell you. At the Greyhound Bus station, just a few miles away from the breakdown.

I was so happy to see him, to have someone to share in the driving that I would have kissed his feet.

After just a few days, I think I began suffering from Stockholm syndrome, or "capture-bonding." For the uninitiated, this is a psychological phenomenon in which hostages express empathy and can develop positive feelings toward their vacation captors, sometimes to the point of identifying with them or even standing up for them. I guess that's why I defended him when the girls told me they had secretly nicknamed him The Velociraptor, or "V-Man" for short after watching him track parking lots for spots like an eagle, or in this case a dinosaur, for its prey.

46

Geronimo!

"Dust everywhere. It traveled in my boots,
swirled up my nose, and came out in black
clumps when I sneezed. It clung to metallic
surfaces and permeated my clothes, rising in
the clouds when I pounded it out. Right now,
I was concerned about its presence on the
bike chain."

—Excerpted from Mark's journals

Many beautiful sprinkles and a smuggling of Mark later, we
landed in Canada (technically, we landed in Nova Scotia after
taking a ferry from St. John's).

"Come on, girls. Time to go tidal bore rafting!" I called out,
jumping into the white-water Zodiac, ready to ride the eleven-foot
waves as the world's highest tides turned the Bay of Fundy into a
cascading water roller coaster. The guide said the walls of water can
reach 53 feet in places and that 160 billion tons of water moved in and
out of the bay twice a day—more than the combined flow of all the
freshwater rivers on our planet.

If you really think about it, what could be cooler than *that?*
Answer? Nothing!

Next it was head first down a thirty-five-foot embankment straight into the Shubenacadie River. "This is awesome!" Nell called out to me (and Mark). "Come on! You gotta try it!"

Mud sliding is like body sledding; and really, what's more fun than body sledding? Plus, the mud's probably good for your complexion (though certainly not for HaRVey's).

"Adam-12" a.k.a. Robbie wasn't much into mud sliding but was a good sport about standing on the sidelines for a good forty-five minutes until we were completely exhausted and covered in brown goo.

Thanks to his hyper-sensitive regard for energy and ecological conservation, Robbie had an issue with water—our water—the water we would use to shower with! He hadn't wanted to waste fuel by driving around with the extra weight in the holding tank. That's why he had emptied it, to save gas.

So now not only didn't we have water, but mud was drying and caking in places you only read about in biology books.

Not to worry, Robbie had a "better" plan. He would obtain "local knowledge" to find water, a practice I previously found amusing, but now made me want to punch him.

Without fail, the obtaining of "local knowledge" entailed the girls and me sitting idle for twenty minutes while he casually chatted with a stranger on the street to find out what was happening on the "local scene." Robbie and his new "informant" would then branch off into all kinds of other subjects, like geothermal heat or what time of year was perfect for growing beefsteak tomatoes. He would then forget which way we were supposed to go or the name of the place we were trying to find. But he would be able to recite the tomato sauce recipe.

This time, however, we scored directions to a campground with showers about five kilometers up the road—which in Nova Scotia really means another fifteen kilometers away.

As the RV bounced along the way, more thick mud cracked off our skin onto the floor. It quickly spread to just about every surface, plastic and upholstery alike. The floor turned clay red—not a speck of white linoleum showed through. We could have at least cleaned it up—but Robbie had tossed the handheld vacuum cleaner, as well.

"Every ounce of weight counts," he said proudly, like I was supposed to be happy that he threw away the vacuum cleaner.

Before reaching the campground, we spotted a car wash. It made sense to the girls and me; we would refill HaRVey's water tank, flip the hot water switch, and have at the clay. Robbie, however, decided the mud might clog the pipes, and suggested that we just hose down in the actual car wash bay with one of those handheld wand sprayers.

You know, the ones meant for washing your car, *not* your daughters.

"No way!" we yelled, taking cover inside the RV. "We're not coming out and you can't make us!"

There was no way I was allowing my kids to stand there being sprayed down with a power washer and especially when the power washer ran on recycled water—as in used car wash water. Surely it was grimy and contained pig poop run off from the hog lagoons that lined the road.

The garden hose was a much better idea, I told Robbie. At least the water was clean for God's sake.

Mark got a bath; and a sprinkle...

47

Memory Lane

"The town had started to change again,
especially the wharf. Gone are the locals
that manifested themselves here during the
tourist season. In their place, a pseudo-
authentic shopping center for the nice
clean middle class has sprung up. Creeping
commercialism, a 70s legacy, finds a host
body in the heart of the land."

—Excerpted from Mark's journals

After that, we made a brief stop in Charlottetown, and then it was off to explore Prince Edward Island.

By this point in our second-annual Tour de Mark, we were old pros. Sure, there were plenty of near-misses and a few debacles, but not counting the whole Southwest wildfire detour thing, there were no major problems. That's a lot more than you can say for my first family RV adventure that had taken place back in the mid-70s.

It was a few years after my father left that my mother took me, my sister Wendy, and our brother Ted to Prince Edward Island in what else, but an RV? I remember the landscape being pastoral with rolling hills, woods, reddish-white sand beaches, and beautiful ocean coves perfect for swimming.

But then a ferry strike turned our one-week vacation into almost three.

I recall it as an almost post-apocalyptic still life image of a single, split-open bag of flour on the floor of an otherwise empty grocery store after ravenous hordes of fellow strandees had stripped the shelves bare.

Campers organized into teams with specific daily assignments to steal apples from orchards, pick wild edible berries and roots from the woods, and to fish off the piers. Then, we all shared in the cooking and eating. It probably wasn't the vacation my Mom had hoped for, but it was certainly a thrilling adventure for us kids.

When the strike finally ended, it took another four days of waiting, waiting, and more waiting in a seven-mile-long line of vehicles before we could board the ferry to go home.

A lot had changed. The island now featured the addition of billboards and strip malls amid the family-run grocery stores and the bait shops I remembered. But by far the most obvious development was that "Anne of Green Gables" mania had taken over the island, with tourists from as far away as Japan shelling out for Anne pens and t-shirts, jams and chocolate-covered PEI potato chips. We too visited "Anne's house" which became one of our favorite places of all.

I hadn't realized how similar our family trips were. My mom and I looked almost identical, too. She was heartbroken, I was heartbroken; she was searching, I was searching; she was in her mid-40's, I was in my mid-40's...

She got over it, I'd get over it.

48
And on His Farm, There Was A...

"What is wrong with you, you ask. Why not just
say it? Tell her how you feel? Is it fear of
rejection? Shyness? Insecurity? Or fear of a
large dog?"

—Excerpted from Mark's journals

V-man Robbie *shockingly* didn't have the phone number or address written down. Maybe the paper weighed too much, so he threw that away, too? Other than knowing it was to be on a farm in Cape Breton and that the bride's mother in law to be had goats, he couldn't remember a single helpful detail—not even the family name.

Robbie proudly put his "local knowledge" plan to work by flagging down anyone and everyone we saw, asking if they knew anything about an upcoming wedding on a goat farm. Details emerged, and soon enough we were pulling up a long road to find a hilltop farmhouse with pretty gardens and a sagging red barn.

"We heard you're afraid of dogs," said the groom's brother, Ken, upon greeting us.

It was nice of Robbie to have forewarned someone of my little phobia.

"Just don't get excited when Rexy comes up to you, is all," he advised. "Just stand tall and brave."

He then quickly realized that telling me to stand up to a dog was like telling a skydiver that the frayed rip cord had just been mended by his elderly grandmother. By hand.

"What happens when you encounter a dog?" he asked with a mixture of concern and amusement.

There was no need to answer. My kids did it for me.

"She pees her pants!" they screamed in unison.

The look on his face was unmistakable. It said, "Please, don't do that here."

He reminded me so much of Mark at that moment, if I peed my pants, it would be over him, not the dog.

I quickly refocused, stammering about how I had been mauled by a German Shepherd at age fourteen and never really got over it. If a dog came running up to me or growled, it was all over...my pants.

As if on cue, Rexy came barreling through the field to eat me alive.

The first thing I saw was the head. It was wide, very wide. Next came the teeth and drooling jowls, which flapped in the wind created by the force of her massive body hurtling through the field. Her gait was a little lopsided; she looked like Old Yeller coming at us, all crazy-like. *Who's got the gun?* I thought wildly. *Shoot the dog. She must have got bit by a rabid coon and she'll eat them young 'uns if you don't kill her, Ken. Kids, don't watch! Close your eyes! Daddy's got the gun!*

Now on the verge of a full-blown bladder incident, I gamely stood my ground. As quickly as the dog landed at my feet, she was jumping up to suck the thyroid right out of my throat.

"Down," commanded Ken.

It wasn't until Rexy flopped herself at our feet and rolled over on her back that I realized she only had three legs. That's why her gait was off.

"Don't worry," Ken said, guiding my hand over the dog's head to pet it. He looked up, smiling, as if to say, "Told you there was nothing to worry about."

You don't need to be Sigmund Freud to analyze what triggered my dream about Mark that night. Being around Ken was almost like being around Mark, only a back-in-the day, much younger, when-we-first-met Mark. A before-he-got-sick Mark.

Maybe this would be like one of those blockbuster love stories where Jennifer Aniston falls in love with someone thirteen years her junior at a stranger's wedding, on a goat farm 997 miles from home.

Being on the farm was good for us. It slowed us down, forced us to wait for things that would normally make me freak out—like how it sometimes took more than twenty minutes to find a cell phone signal.

And healthy, too; out here, the air was so clean you could taste it. Living off the land, getting dirt under un-manicured fingernails, drying laundry on the line instead of in a machine; just me, my girls, new friends. It felt good to be here, and that was just right for right now.

Pretty soon, I learned the farm's one-eyed rooster wasn't the only early riser in the family. Monique, the boys' mother, was up each day at 6:00 am, taking care of what needed to be done around the farm. It was obvious that Martha Stewart didn't live here, but she could keep her fancy chickens and perfect pastures. Monique rocked.

That's actually one of the first conversations we had, about how she managed to do everything herself, except when the boys visited for a month every summer. Also, about her stroke. She could no longer multi-task and had to walk with directed purpose to overcome her balance issues, which could sometimes still tip her over, she said. But the thing is you'd never know it unless she told you.

Goat milking was at 7:30 am, and I made sure the girls were up and at 'em. Not that there was much to it: Step one, turn on the TV (which makes the milking go by more quickly); step two, milk the goat.

"Just take the teat and close it off here, then wrap your fingers around it and gently squeeze, like this," she said, expertly expressing a stream of rich milk.

The girls had waited a lifetime for an opportunity like this, and Monique soon trusted us to milk the goats on our own. After about an hour, she called us into the house. In came the baked goods, and out went my diet; those cinnamon buns were too gooey and too good to pass up.

The porch was the best place to enjoy our treats while looking out across the pastures and Bras d'Or Lake with its magnificent sheer cliffs, all stitched together under a purple palette sky.

Monique poured me a cup of tea. "Goat milk?" she offered, as casually as a hunter might say, "12- or 20-gauge?"

I really didn't want goat milk in my tea. We had just got through shaving one of the goat's hairy teat clefts before milking it, joking about giving them Brazilian bikini waxes. How was I supposed to put that image out of my mind?

"Oh, yes please." I heard the words coming from my mouth as she poured the white liquid into our mugs.

"Sugar?" she asked sweetly.

"No, thank you," I replied.

I looked at her. She looked at me. I sipped. She sipped.

"It's delicious. Thank you," I managed.

A proud smile slid across her face.

Next, Monique went off to slaughter a few meat birds for dinner. Another simple process, she said: Step one, grab the bird by the throat; step two, slit deeply; step three, eviscerate. Then, you just toss the entrails in the bucket.

There was no outsourcing the difficult jobs and no separating yourself from the cycles of life and death on the farm. Sure, you could respect and even love a chicken while it was living. But after you killed it for dinner, tossed the body in a pot of boiling water, and plucked out every single feather to make it look neat and pretty, you simply had to live with the knowledge that you were eating the cute black and white one.

At dinner, I'm pretty sure I was the only one chewing through clenched teeth to keep from saying the chicken's name out loud.

(I'll tell you: it was Gertrude.)

Life on the farm may have been brutally to the point, but I liked how simple things like taking the garbage out or borrowing a neighbor's tractor became an event.

The following day, as the men threw homegrown bales of hay onto a conveyor belt contraption that moved it to the second floor of the barn, Monique and I prepared lunch and baked berry pies. I tried not to watch Ken through the window and was never so glad when the pies came out of the oven.

When he stepped into the kitchen, we ate and chatted for more than an hour. (I know because that's about how long it takes to muck the stalls).

Why, oh why did he have to have the same mannerisms as Mark?

Later, when we took a walk on the beach together, Ken stopped short, bending down to pick something up.

"It's beautiful," he said, thumbing a piece of blue sea glass in his hand. "Like the color of your eyes. Deep, sparkling blue."

Returning his gaze, I told him they're called mermaid tears.

He took my hand and opened it with his, pressing the smooth glass into my palm before closing it over the treasure. He didn't let go, and I didn't pull away. We stood there for a moment, aware of our bodies dancing to our breath, pulsing in the sun.

"Laura, you are a beautiful mermaid."

He tilted my head toward his and kissed me. "It's okay. You are home now," he whispered protectively in my ear. "Stay. Stay here with me."

"Ken," I managed breathlessly, feeling the tingle of his face against mine...

Snap! I had fallen asleep in a lawn chair, dreaming of Mark—or was it Ken? Only, it was Rexy, happily nuzzling my face to wake me up.

Then came the simple yet elegant outdoor wedding ceremony, followed by the reception at a beautiful waterfront restaurant. Later, we all gathered at the beach for a bonfire, roasting marshmallows and drinking champagne straight from the bottle.

I really wanted Mark to share in the moment.

Within seconds, the fire began snapping and popping. Mark's ashes had begun to explode in hot fire pops.

"Ouch! What was that?" Ken cried, swatting at the back of his neck.

"Ow!" the bride called out.

"Mommy, something is burning me," cried Susannah, smacking at her leg.

"What is going on with that fire?" the groom demanded, putting out the burning hole in the sleeve of his sport coat.

How could I possibly explain that I thought it appropriate to put a dead man's ashes in their wedding bonfire? What was wrong with me?

Thankfully, Gregory suggested that the flaming spitballs were probably flecks of brick mortar. My secret was safe.

The girls and I would have been happy to stay at the farm all summer long, but it was time to go.

There were hugs all around.

Off we drove, honking the horn and waving out the windows.

There was no reason for the sudden rush of doom and gloom I felt overtake me as the farm disappeared from view. *Just breathe,* I told myself as my heart began thumping.

Breathe through your nose, Laura. Breathe through your nose. A closed mouth, with the tongue placed up the palate ensures that the breathing happens in and out the nose. Now, Laura. Extend the exhale. That's it. It will be okay. You will get through it. Just breathe.

It's been close to two years, I told myself. *Your husband is dead. You have devised this ridiculous ritual of spreading his ashes because the truth is, you can't let go. You're prolonging it because you are too afraid to face life without him. It's kind of sick to keep his underwear in your drawer. You continue to wear them sometimes, too. What is that about? And you're still sleeping with his ashes. You talk about him in the present tense. You haven't taken off your rings. You keep distracting yourself. Running away instead of dealing with it.*

Now, concentrate on your heart rate. Slow it down. Down. Down. It's not a heart attack. You're not going to the emergency room. It's just a panic attack. Get back up. You are strong. You have to do this.

Breathe. Sprinkle. And breathe some more.

49

Canada, OH Canada

"A thousand lives, Jon, ten thousand! And then
another hundred lives until we began to learn
that there is such a thing as perfection,
and another hundred again to get the idea
that our purpose for living is to find that
perfection and show it forth. The same rule
holds for us now, of course: we choose our
next world through what we learn in this one.
Learn nothing and the next world is the same
as this one, all the same limitations and
lead weights to overcome."

—From Mark's journal, excerpted from *Jonathan
Livingston Seagull*

The Canadian roads were long and picturesque. Sometimes it was just us and the mountains, on and on to infinity. Other times, the hillsides were framed with charming houses surrounding little villages with white church steeples.

One morning in Tadoussac, a small fishing town on the Saguenay Fjord in Northern Quebec, I scrambled out over the mossy boulders at the water's edge in hopes of catching some whale action. It felt serene out there, with only the sound of lapping waves under a dark blanket of sky, though walking alone on the beach made it easy to wallow in self-pity. That happens to everyone, doesn't it? That feeling of insignificance when standing at the ocean's edge?

I lifted the binoculars to get a better look at a ripple in the water that became surrounded by a noticeable flat spot. Could it be? Was it? Yes! A whale surfaced, its black back slithering along before suddenly shooting through the water as it arched and bowed before going back under, out of sight.

A seagull landed nearby. It stood there, watching me place a handful of ashes in between two boulders where seawater pooled into a cave.

"What do *you* want?" I asked it out loud.

The bird didn't move, and neither did I.

It was a stare down of souls.

Its sudden departure back into the sky left me somewhat spiritually shaken. Was the bird really Mark, telling me to set myself free? To make one with myself? To become the bird? To be the bird?

The thought stayed with me throughout the next sprinkles: Baddeck, Ingonish, Belle Cote, Chéticamp, Dingwall, Cape North, Fredericton, and New Brunswick. There was so much stunning nature to be seen, so many opportunities to appreciate the moment and practice letting go.

But it wasn't all poignant and bittersweet.

"Look, kids. There's a bright yellow flower field. Do you think Daddy would like to rest there?"

"No, Mommy, over here," Nell insisted, sitting down on a rock to dip her bare feet into the water.

"It's my turn, not yours!" Susannah shrieked.

"No, it's not. You got to sprinkle him at the car dealership yesterday," her sister reminded her.

It's true. I pretended to be in the market for a Fiat just to sprinkle a little on the stick shift.

"Yes, but that was only after you took *my* turn when we were watching whales!"

"Fermez la bouche!" I yelled so loudly that the seas practically parted. This was the nicest way I knew how tell them to shut up without telling them to shut up—en Français, s'il vous plaît.

Poor Robbie. It was one of the few times I felt sorry for him. He either wished that he had his own family to take across Canada, or else he was very, very glad that he hadn't.

But enough feeling sorry for him. I jokingly told him to suck it up, that he deserved every bit of us for not sticking to the original travel plan.

Onward, Pittmans!

50

No "Hélicoptère" for You, Madame

"Fear, man. That's for the castrated. Me and
you, we've got better things to do. Go to
the top of the mountain. Life runs on razor
blades, thin ice and motorcycles."

—Excerpted from Mark's journals

Mark always called me Lucky Laura.

Put me in Times Square twenty minutes before show time, and I'll find free street parking. Enter a raffle and I'll win it. Tell me to go to hell, and I'll wave to you from heaven.

But get it in my head to go rock climbing just so I could sprinkle Mark from 1,400 feet in the air?

Not so lucky.

Of course, almost everything sounds like a good idea to Lucy. She especially likes the adventurous ones where she can overcome some quasi-phobia or intense fear; all the better to juice up the emotional power pack. If she could overcome open water swimming and drooling dogs, why not heights?

We were at Les Palissades, the hot spot for rock climbing in the Saint-Siméon Charlevoix Region. The guide handed us bags of chalk to get better grips on the rope. He spoke little English and I could only communicate in the equivalent of kindergarten French, but all that mattered was him not seeing me sneak a handful of Mark into the bag.

It's probably for the best that the guide couldn't hear the exchange between Nell and me when we got halfway up the mountain too. That's where I suddenly froze; my body would not move. He and Susannah were way up there, *along* with the rest of the group. And we were way, way down here, *away* from the rest of the group.

"Come on Mom. You can do it. You have to," Nell said in her determined, very mature way.

"But I can't, Nell. I can't...make it," I whimpered, clinging to the side of a three-foot ledge. *Just don't look down; whatever you do, Laura, don't look down.* And what did I stupidly do? Looked down. The two massive lodges had morphed into a miniature village with dollhouse-sized log cabins and tiny little people driving tiny little cars around a tiny little bathtub-looking lake. That's how far we were off the ground. It was nauseating.

Nell continued to coax, in hopes of making it look easy or fun or something. Let me tell you. It was none of the above. It is the most terrifying feeling on earth to realize you're dangling 1200 feet in the air *and* that it's your own fault.

"Mom, you have to snap out of it," Nell insisted, holding her hand out for me to grab onto as I cried. "Do you want me to get Daddy?"

"Yes," I gasped. "Get him. I need him." Only, that meant twisting my waist toward her, so she could reach into the bag of chalk attached to my hip. What if I slipped? The answer was simple. I'd fall and die.

She smartly and swiftly grabbed the chalk bag from my belt loop. Major...massive...sprinkle...all...over...the...rock...

"Look, Mom. There he is. Dad's on the ledge right by your feet," she said, tossing another handful for good measure. "He's here now, and if I can do this and Susannah can do this and even he can do this, then *you* can do this. Just move your leg three inches. Let me see you wiggle your foot."

"You okay?" the guide had appeared out of nowhere, landing at our feet like Spiderman to the rescue. Only he was standing in the pile of ash and began dusting it off his boots, then wiping his hands on his pants, leaving prints. "Chalk for hands to climb mountain, not for thrown on ground."

"Hey, that's my Dad," Nell said, but quickly quieted.

"You not okay?" he asked me again.

"No, how could I be okay?" I felt like saying. "If I were okay, do you think I would be climbing this mountain in the first place? I am afraid of heights, dude, and I'm trying to prove something to myself here, but it's not working out so well, is it? So when you ask me if I'm ok and I tell you no, I am not ok, I mean it. I AM NOT OK! I'm the furthest from okay that I've ever been in my life!"

No further conversation was necessary...now that I had just thrown up all over the man's boots.

"Oh my God, she is so sorry," Nell offered with a mixture of complete disgust and embarrassment, explaining that I am normally not a boot-puker; just someone who is "really, really, really afraid of heights."

"Why you make mountain?" he asked, scraping the remnants of my eggs Benedict onto a rock.

"That's a great question, Mom. Why did you make mountain?" Nell asked mockingly. "What were you possibly thinking? You know you don't make mountain. You can't even make Ferris wheel. Why mountain?"

Foam drooling from my mouth now, the only words I could say were "Hel-i-copter. I need a hel-i-copter."

"Oh! Hélicoptère!" the guide said excitedly. "You need hélicoptère?"

We were finally getting somewhere. Hopefully, that somewhere was off this mountain.

"Yes, a rescue hel-i-copter. I need a rescue hel-i-copter."

He shook his head. "No hélicoptère for you, Madame. You make climb with kids." Translated: He had to carry me on his back the rest of the way up.

I can't say I felt triumphant spreading Mark from the treetops on that mountain—or from the 200-meter suspension bridge hanging 656 feet in the air. You know, the one that we had to walk across in order to hike back down the mountain. It was either that or rappel down. *No thanks. I'd really rather die.*

Later, I learned that sufficiently traumatic events cause an overactive adrenaline response, as well as the secretion of high levels of those pesky stress hormones. This chemical soup not only suppresses hypothalamic activity, it also creates deep neurological patterns in the brain that can persist long after the trigger.

What this means is I am now basically scarred for life after making mountain for Mark.

We found hard ground touring around in Quebec City and then in Montreal. After a brief stopover in the Thousand Islands, we headed to Rochester so the girls could see the house where I grew up.

How did our apple trees get so big? I remembered helping to plant them as little twigs. Look girls, there's my bedroom window. Only, now it has different curtains.

I laid down in the grass that was now a stranger's lawn, thinking about how quickly it all goes.

Still, some people believe that the spirit lives on until the last person left on earth who knew him or her dies. There's another philosophy that a child is born with all of its intelligence and wisdom, only to lose a bit as each year passes.

Taken together, I guess it's true: the older you get, the more life you forget, and the more life forgets you.

Then, the real question becomes, 'RV there yet?'

"What's wrong?" Susannah asked, offering me a taste of her ice cream. I had allowed the girls to walk across the street to the dairy.

"I think I just...want to go home," I admitted. I tried not to cry in front of the girls but sometimes I couldn't help it. "Maybe it's best to just be done. Just hide Daddy in the wheel well and sell the RV." That way he could keep on trucking while we stayed put.

According to Dave at the Camping World RV Superstore in Syracuse NY, our little 21-foot Class C Toyota Dolphin was a "highly sought-after vehicle."

"People would kill for this," he remarked, touring HaRVey with a little too much enthusiasm. He especially liked the layout and kept saying how people loved retro campers.

"You really want to sell it? I'll buy it from you right now, and pay for your rental car home," he offered. "Or, if you'd like, go on and finish your trip and I can arrange for someone to come pick it up from you at your convenience. No extra charge."

While all of this was good news, I suddenly didn't want anyone else to have him. HaRVey was ours! I couldn't imagine him driving with any other family. We were just homesick.

Of course, the bigger consideration was that we had no real home to be sick for. Our old house was pretty much boxed up and the new house would still feel unfamiliar. For better or for worse, HaRVey was the closest thing we had to a "home." And we loved him for it.

We treated him to a car wash and spent a few hours doing a deep clean to make up for even thinking of selling him.

"We love you HaRVey, oh yes we do," we sang. "We love you HaRVey, and we'll be true."

Part V:
Looking for
Love

51

This Old-New House, This New-Old Life

"Food. Between us, we always ate. Well, most
of the time, anyway. Condensed soup mostly
straight from the can."

—Excerpted from Mark's journals

"**W**e're home!" I called back to the girls as we pulled into the driveway of our new hovel.

The inspector's report had come in via email while we were at a cafe in Canada. It was twenty-seven pages long, citing everything from a cracked foundation to major plumbing issues, to say nothing of the slanting floors, electrical problems, mold, no insulation, broken windows, water damage, broken tiles and drywall, or the 1960s-era kitchen appliances.

You name it, it was broken, cracked, stained, or non-functioning. I knew going in that you get what you pay for, but *I swear* I really didn't understand just how bad it was. And it was too late now.

Look at the bright side, Laura. At least it isn't on wheels!

"This is our new house?" Nell moaned as we plowed over a runway of weeds to get into the driveway. "Mom? Tell me you're kidding. This is it?"

"You don't expect us to live in this, do you?" Susannah railed.

They were all for it when I showed it to them in person before; excited, even. But you know how kids are—sometimes they don't make obvious connections. When you buy a house, that means you own it *and* it means you live in it, come hell or no running water.

"No freaking way. I refuse. It's creepy and gross and I will never live here," they continued.

It really wasn't that bad, I told them (and myself). It just needs some work—a whole lot of work.

By now, I was worried—seriously worried—that I—not Lucy or the Bad Girl Scout, *me*—had finally made the biggest mistake of my life. For better or worse, there was no way we could go back to our real house, the nice one. I'd rented it to a sparkling young pregnant couple. It was now their happy home. And this was ours.

It was a good thing we didn't sell HaRVey. We had no place to go otherwise; at least this way, we could be homeless in our own safely secluded driveway.

First things first. I needed a cigarette (just one, I promise).

"Well, look who came back!" Deli Man was practically jumping up and down. "Now, where did you go this time? You have not been to see me in a long time."

I told him we went to see the Queen, but he didn't get the joke.

His eyes got big. "You went to England?"

This really made me laugh. "No, no, that's an American expression. Never mind. How's everything?" I truly did want to know how he had been. It had been more than a month since we had seen each other, and I'd kind of missed my swami.

He waved his hand as though to dismiss the question. "Tell me. How was your vacation? Are you ready to move?" he asked.

It wasn't a matter of being ready; it was more whether we were capable of handling the move. That night, I plopped Mark's tools down in front of the girls and explained that the harder they worked on their rooms, the faster they would finish, and the sooner they could move into them.

This entailed cutting up and ripping out the thirty-year-old wall-to-wall pet-stained carpeting throughout the whole upstairs and then using pliers to pull out all the tacks. I bought the girls matching pink drills at Home Depot to remove the hundreds of screws holding the plywood to reach (what I thought was) the finished wood flooring underneath, hoping that would further motivate them.

Oops!

Live and learn, I guess. It turned out to be subfloor, the raw wood used to construct a house. There was nothing "finished" about it. But it was too late, the DIY damage had been done.

Rather than spend thousands on installing hardwood, we simply painted the floors white.

"I know it's hard," I continued, urging them on. "That's why it's called work and that's why fun is called fun. But you can make work fun, you know. Come on, girls, we can do this. Let's have fun!"

The mistakes went on from there, starting with the kitchen. When I pulled out the ugly old cabinets, the wall came down with them. When we removed the ceramic floor tiles by sledgehammer, the fragments stuck to the glue. When the kitchen sink cracked, we had to recruit the garden hose and a bucket.

"Some people don't even *have* running water," I told the girls. "Consider yourselves lucky."

They didn't.

One morning, a few weeks of hell-bound renovations later, I found Susannah on the back deck, wrapped in a sleeping bag eating Campbell's soup...directly from the can and with a plastic fork (there were no spoons left). She called it breakfast.

How was it possible that I had gone from private boarding school to this?

"I hate it here," she moaned. "I want to go home." This didn't seem the time to tell her that plaster dust had fallen off her hair and into her soup.

"But we *are* home, honey," I said as cheerfully as I could. I had no idea it would be this hard or take this long or cost this much. But I knew it would eventually come together.

How long could it possibly take? It was only 1300 sq. feet of space to fix.

"You'll like it here," I continued, trying to persuade her. "New school. New bedroom. Everything. It's our fresh start."

I just hoped none of the kids at school discovered that we were living out of an RV. Not the best way to make new friends, especially in the tony suburbs.

She wasn't convinced. "I miss Dad. If he never died, we would be home in our own beds. And we wouldn't have had to move. Now I'm sleeping in a stupid RV like a homeless person in a horrible house that I hate and...I just want our lives back, Mom. Can't you make Daddy come back? Can we go home now, please? Mom. Take me home. I want to go home," she cried.

I did the only thing I could: I took the girls out for a pancake breakfast the next day at IHOP in the hopes of cheering them up. There's nothing like giant gobs of whipped cream and blueberry syrup to put smiles back on their faces.

After a full day of nothing but fun, I went out to the driveway with Mark after putting the girls to bed. Leaning against HaRVey, I opened the lid to his box in the hopes the fresh air would wake him up. We needed to talk.

"Mark, can you please let me know if you can hear me? I've learned all the lessons I need to. I will never yell at you for machine washing and ruining all my 'dry clean only' clothes ever again. Okay, I further promise not to freak out when you don't call to tell me you're on your way home, just so I can gauge whether you are truly late or truly dead. Or how about I promise to volunteer at a homeless shelter? Or I can donate blood every week. Maybe break cement blocks with my bare hands? Please God, can't you send him back to us? The girls need him here much more than you need him there."

The next day we went to see Candice at the plumbing supply store. You make good friends with people who work at plumbing stores at times like these.

She handed me a piece of paper. "Here. This is Sam's number; call him. He's the best."

He was also the worst. Actually, Pete—who I hired to hoist up the sagging house—was the worst, but for different reasons. At least Sam showed up; Porno Pete, which is what Sam called him, rarely did. Sam knew his trade, whereas PP seemed to be learning on the job—*my* job.

There was one other big difference between the two: Porno Pete never proposed to me, whereas Sam did—complete with a copper plumbing pipe he had cut into a ring. I didn't think he was serious until his wife called screaming and yelling at me the next morning. He didn't come to work after that, and I've never seen him since.

But at least neither of them was thieves, which doesn't sound like much of a selling point, until it means everything.

I hired a new round of so-called professionals, the worst of the worst. They were slow, they were sloppy, and if I wasn't there to supervise, nothing got done. Even then, what *did* get done was typically done wrong and needed redoing.

Fine, I thought. *I'll do it my-freaking-self.* That's what miter saws, nail guns, and YouTube videos are for, right? What I could do, I *would* do. And did.

But there were still things requiring manly labor, like hanging drywall or installing light fixtures. During one of those times, I put my big chunky silver bracelet and my beautiful wedding rings in the medicine cabinet for safekeeping before painting the new walls. When I went retrieve the jewelry about six hours later, the bracelet was still there, but the rings were gone.

The police said there was nothing I could do but file a report and hope they turned up. Meanwhile, the contractor threatened to kill the worker he suspected of stealing the rings, which was thoughtful, I guess, but not really helpful.

I changed the locks and spent the next few weeks emailing pictures of the rings to every police station and pawn shop in the Tri-State area.

I still walk into every pawn shop I pass, looking for them, even today. I know they're out there somewhere.

52

That's What Friends
Are For

"I saw her on the back of the bike and I
knew why they'd brought her to meet me. The
beautiful girl with electric blue eyes. I
had to ask her name three times. Man, could
she shoot pool. We played doubles with the
guys in polyester suits, shirts opened to the
navel and zodiac signs on medallions around
their necks."

—Excerpted from Mark's journals

My friends decided they knew just what—or who—would make everything better.

Or at least be able to install the new Wolf stove I bought at an auction.

"Freddy," my friend Lisa said, smiling. "He can do the gas line work, and you can meet him. As in, *meet* him."

"Who's Freddy?" I asked, sensing something was up. "Oh, wait. Don't tell me. You mean to date? You want to fix me up with a contractor? No way. I'm not interested in dating *anyone*, especially a contractor." I took a bite of a frosted pumpkin cookie and followed it with a big sip of Chardonnay.

"Freddy's a really good friend of mine. Trust me," Lisa insisted. She gestured nearby, to where Barb was sitting. "He's done work for Barb too." Barb nodded, smiling. "He's a plumber, but he also built his own house. Himself."

The three of us were standing in the kitchen at a kids' Halloween party. That's what you do in the suburbs: you have Halloween parties for kids and hang out in the kitchen drinking wine with the other moms.

That's nice, but I didn't care how smart or sweet or scrupulous this "Freddy" was, I was not about to call him to put in my stove or anything else. So what if it had been four years since Mark died. I was doing just fine on my own.

One morning several months later, however, I had no other choice. There was *something* that smelled like a dead skunk or a rotting refrigerator coming from the basement. Upon opening the door to investigate, I was greeted by a floor full of sewer water—the brown kind that comes from hundreds of houses on top of the hill with everything that gets flushed, toilet paper, baby wipes, tampons, and towels—you name it—swimming on the floor.

Unlike any other contractor I had ever worked with, Freddy actually showed up—and on time! Which was just in time to see me spraying my boots clean with the garden—I mean kitchen—hose.

Freddy told me not to worry, that he would cap the spewing pipe and have an emergency clean-up crew in and out by the time I got home from work. There was something about him that made me trust him immediately. And when he said to call him anytime as I rushed out the door to work, I knew he didn't mean just for plumbing disasters.

I texted Lisa and Barb from the train platform. "Freddy is cute. And nice. And smart. I had to leave him—am on train to city for work."

Seconds later, the iPhone pinged.

"Take it easy, Cupcake," the text read. "I'm glad you think I'm cute and nice and smart. So are you."

It took a minute to realize that I had responded to a three-way text—which had included Freddy!

53

A Little to the Left

"Alone in this frozen place, humanity calls
home. Patience, patience. It's something
we've all known. The stage is set for rescue.
The moon is full. She is in your sight."

—Excerpted from Mark's journals

When the ceiling sprung a leak a few months later, so did I.
It wasn't so much an issue of faulty plumbing this time; the
bathroom sink I installed myself was now leaking.

Less than an hour and a bucket full of water later, Freddy stood
in the doorway, smiling.

"Told you you'd call me," he teased.

A whole season had gone by since the sewage incident. The girls
were totally settled. My brain cells had miraculously regenerated (for
the most part), so work was going better. We even had a beautiful new
kitchen.

This time, though, I wasn't rushing out the door. It was a
Saturday—no meetings, no school, no orthodontist appointments. I
was free to be his plumber's helper.

I could do that now; I could hold engaging conversations about
wax toilet seals, pipe snaking tips, and how best to re-drywall the

now-crumbling ceiling in addition to the regular stuff like where we grew up and who we voted for.

We chatted the whole time he worked, me sitting on the edge of the tub and him with his head wedged under the sink. I tried hard not to be attracted to him but had forgotten how much I liked Levi's jeans.

"Hand me that screwdriver?" he asked. "And use the other one to tighten the bolt up there."

I was trying.

"Okay, screw it harder," he joked, as I twisted it against the pipe. Freddy was teaching me to fish!

"A little to the left," he instructed, obviously enjoying my embarrassed laughter.

"Do I hold it here or there?" I asked, not realizing the implications of my words.

"Hold it anyway you like," he fired back.

A few hours later, after insisting on helping me fix a bunch of other things, he turned and kissed me.

"I've been wanting to do that since we met," he said, laughing to himself in a "I-can't-believe-I-just-did-that" kind of way. "If I could have made that leak happen myself, you know I would have just to see you again. I like you, Laura."

I liked him, too.

That night, we did something I hadn't done in years: shot pool and drank beer at a local dive bar.

And, absolutely unbelievably, "American Pie" came on the jukebox just as we walked in the bar.

54

Lies, Lies and More Lies

"Didn't have a camera by my side this time, hoping I would see the world through both my eyes, not inside a picture frame. It brought me back to life."

—Excerpted from Mark's journals

Being with Freddy was like reuniting with an old friend; we just had a lot of catching up to do.

The girls didn't realize we had started seeing each other. They must have thought we just had a lot of plumbing problems.

That's what led to my current dilemma: how was I supposed to tell them I would be spending the weekend at his country house? No way. It would be better for everyone if I said I'd been called to an out-of-town conference.

"Here, wear my scarf, Mommy. It looks so pretty on you," Susannah said, wrapping it around my neck with fashion flair as we packed my weekend bag. She's always been really good at accessorizing. "And don't worry, Mom. We'll be fine."

It was my first time leaving them overnight with a babysitter. I already felt guilty.

But once I got on the road, with the radio blasting, windows and moon roof wide open, I felt freer than I had in forever.

While out celebrating Nell's birthday a few nights later, the girls were looking through our trip pictures on my iPhone, when Nell suddenly shouted, "Look, it's Freddy!" while shoving the phone in her sister's face so she could see him, too. "And he's wearing your scarf!"

I grabbed the phone, hoping to hide the evidence, but it was too late. There was Freddy, wearing Susannah's blue scarf. Or, to be more specific, there was Freddy, *blindfolded* by her blue scarf.

Then they both burst into tears—just as the birthday cake arrived.

I swear all I did was blindfold him and whisper, you know, really hot things in his ear; things like, "So, tell me, Ferdinando...do you like Fritos or Doritos? Skiing or snowboarding? Hemingway or Harry Potter?" For each "right answer" I'd pop a chocolate chip in his mouth.

That was it—the extent of our pretend kink—but the photo made it look so...so much worse.

The girls were rightfully horrified, especially since they would prefer I shroud myself in black until keeling over at the age of ninety-two than ever see me go out with a man and especially a man with their scarf tied over his eyes.

"You *lied*, Mom," Susannah said, wounded. "You said you were going out of town, and you were really with Freddy."

It was then I realized that not telling them the truth had its own consequences.

And that I should put a password on my phone.

55

Deli Man
to the Rescue

"It was an unusual thing to see. This pairing
of souls. From the looks of it, they seemed
to dig on Dostoevsky's philosophy, numb to
the contingent realities around them."

—Excerpted from Mark's journals

The transition from born again virgin to sleeping with Freddy to
getting caught sleeping with Freddy called for a cigarette.
Straight to the deli, then.

"I need to get some eggs for breakfast," I lied. I was getting good
at this!

"I don't understand it," said Deli Man, shaking his head. "You
are very smart, I know. You are a good mother. You are a healthy and
beautiful and kind woman. Why?"

"Why what?" I asked. "Why am I sneaking a cigarette?"

"No. Why are you single?" he said.

How does he *do* that? "What makes you think I am single?"

"Because you still have sadness deep in yourself. I can see it."

Here I thought I was showing major improvement, and he says I still look sad? Wasn't being with Freddy living proof that I was better?

I told Deli Man that I didn't need a man to be happy. "No one can make another person happy. They can add to your life, but they can't complete you." It was true. Look at Freddy. As much as we enjoyed each other's company and truly liked each other, I was still too unhappy to be happy with him... or with anyone. We lasted for a while but realized our relationship would never progress to anything more than what it was.

"That's how you call? Bull?" Deli Man said getting all serious. "I tell you, *everyone* needs someone, and I can see that a man made you very unhappy. For a long time, you have been this way. You need love again. Real love. To heal your heart, you will need love."

"He didn't make me unhappy. I loved him," I told him. This conversation was clearly calling for a second cigarette.

"Why aren't you with him, then?" he asked. "Go find him and tell him you still feel like this for him."

"He died."

"He did? He died?" Deli Man's eyes got misty. Was he really about to cry? "He was your husband?"

"Yes, he was my husband."

"*Now* I know why you are the way you are! Your spirit, it is half-broken."

Without realizing it, I had been plucking the petals off a bouquet of sunflowers as the words twisted inside me: "He loves me. He loves me not. He is breathing. He is breathing not. She is still grieving. She is still grieving not."

56

Table for Two, Please

"The day was long, slow and full of promise.
For what? I don't know, but I could feel it
in the air. The presence was everywhere. I
realized our choices are what shake the webs
that bind humanity."

—Excerpted from Mark's journals

It was September 12 again, and I had a hot date with the love of my life.

It was our 19th wedding anniversary. Mark wore his velvet cufflink bag. I wore his favorite dress (the silver one with pretty flowers) and high heels.

"Are you sure you don't want me to clear the table setting?" the server asked discretely after about ten minutes. It was clear that she thought I had been stood up.

"No, it's fine right where it is," I told her. "Thank you very much."

I was no Emily Grierson, the character from Faulkner's *A Rose for Miss Emily* who leaves her fiancé's rotting corpse locked in her bedroom for years to preserve their relationship.

At least Mark got out of the house.

I became reluctant to visit the Hudson View Deli, knowing how Deli Man would read all of my thoughts and intuit my failures. Other times, I almost liked testing him.

But this was one of those times. It was night, as always, when I stepped out for an American Spirit (and maybe a single beer).

"Love life?" he said, more like an announcement than a question.

I rolled my eyes and groaned.

"You have too much to offer," he told me, waving his hand in the air. "They're no good for you. Get rid of them. The good ones will find you."

I *had* a good one. But the truth was, I wasn't sure I really wanted anyone.

57

Et Voila! No-Cation
Becomes Stay-Cation

"I know it's been a long time. I've never felt
that far away. You were always on my mind,
and now I am home with you, where I will
stay."

—Excerpted from Mark's journals

With summer coming up, everyone was surprised to hear we
wouldn't be taking off again.

We now loved our new house and how it represented our ability
to persevere and make the best of things. We needed to just BE. BE
in the house. BE settled. Plant flower gardens. Sew pretty curtains for
the windows. Paint the house from ugly pinkish-gray to a nice sage
green color. Create happy memories.

BE. BE. BE.

Just as the house painters readied themselves to go up the ladders,
another BIG IDEA hit Lucy.

Sprinkle...then stir big handfuls of Mark in the paint when no one
was looking.

Mark could also get laid, in asphalt and gravel, that is—when we put down a new driveway.

A sprinkle in the flower beds...and now he could grow.

We were feeling the love, the girls and me.

58

Here Today, Gone Tomorrow

"Samuel stood admiring his sunflower
fields. He'd tell Ruth it was like looking
at one thousand suns."

—Excerpted from Mark's journals

"You want to smoke. I can see it," Deli Man said, frowning, as he handed me a cigarette. He was right. It was straight to the refrigerator case for a nice cold Corona, too.

"Why are people so demented? I mean...seriously! What is wrong with the world?!" I demanded.

He looked at a ratty newspaper someone had left on the counter and then he looked at me. "Garbage. It's all garbage. I don't read it. No news for me."

I had noticed he always had a book going. Now I knew why.

"Books are the truth of the mind," he continued. "Newspapers are for the masses. Always bad news."

I didn't tell him I'd worked as a newspaper reporter. Maybe that's why he never told me he was widowed. (Someone else had told me that summer.) I guess that was his secret all along.

It's ironic how two people can find in each other what they need, even in the most unexpected places. Here we were, Deli Man and me, both grieving, both healing in our own ways; no overt effort involved; just two people dealing with their lives, each open to uncomplicated human interaction.

I was careful never to feed him the question that would prompt an answer—or the omission of one—about his late wife. If he didn't want me to know, I didn't want to let on that I knew. Our shared loss was a perfect secret. Even unspoken, it bonded us in a new, intimate-but-not-intimate kind of trust.

HaRVey started winking at me, as if to say, "Come on. Let's continue our mission to ensure Mark can really R.I.P. I know exactly which places to hit! We'll go local, no worries!"

We hit St. Vincent's Hospital, where the kids were born; Bloomberg Headquarters; Mark's favorite bar called The Subway; and the boat house pond in Central Park.

Then we headed north to the newsroom at the Times-Herald Record. Ironically, Hunter Thompson once worked there (until he kicked the vending machine in a fit of anger and got fired); Bethel, where Mark covered Woodstock II; Beaver Dam Lake, where we had our cabin; and Saugerties, where we got married.

We continued sprinklings while taking surfing lessons and going camping on the beach and then hiking in the White Mountains of New Hampshire and visiting Stowe, Vermont. There's something about being in the woods that refocuses your perspective and refreshes your energy. But not this time.

We were out of sorts. And no amount of positive thinking and sprinkling could change it.

This is what you call a turning point. It's when I decided to be the one in charge here and that my response in all situations determines whether a crisis had escalated or de-escalated. I could create the mood and set the example.

With that, we turned HaRVey around and drove straight home to reclaim our happy little house. Came home to reclaim our happy little house. We planted big beautiful flower gardens out front and made three vegetable gardens in the back. We let the sun shine through the open windows. We rode our new bikes and went on picnics by the river. We took back what was ours, including the lawn mower at our old house before the new owners moved in.

Walking the property one last time, I wondered whether the girls would ever come back here, to their childhood home, to sit under the apple trees they had planted when they were little.

As I held up my phone to take one last picture, something caught my eye. A lone sunflower standing big and tall and bright and yellow was growing right there in the middle of the yard. In the nine years we had lived there, we couldn't even grow grass much less flowers.

I fell into a heap. Was it a sign? Had Mark reappeared, leaving behind a sunflower like a message in a bottle? Was he there to show me in this startling and profound way that he had been with us every mile of the way?

These are the crazy coincidences, the inexplicable things that make you want to believe. Because, really, how can you not?

Careful not to damage the roots, I gently dug it out of the ground, then rushed down the front steps to the driveway, where the ambulance workers had taken Mark's body out on the stretcher. I drove past the hospital and then another quarter-mile down the road to our new house.

I made a new home for him in the front garden, lined it with organic soil, and gave him a long drink from a bottle of spring water.

Then, I just sat by its side.

A sunflower's stalk is thick and tall, yet its round face still droops downward under its own weight. Botanists tell us that sunflowers look down to better scatter their own seeds, to see them sprout and grow.

But this was not the case with Mark's sunflower.

At first, I figured it was just weak from the shock of moving to new territory. But day after day, it looked droopier and more fatigued. My friend Kate said not to worry, that sunflowers are one of the hardiest flowers of all; that it just needed time.

"A watched pot never boils," she advised. "It needs to acclimate to its new surroundings." All the same, I could tell the prognosis wasn't good. She had that same worried look that doctors get.

Every day I sat on the porch, watching it the way a mother watches her young.

"Come on, Sunny. You can do it," I encouraged. "All you need to do is hold your head up and grow."

It continued looking weak and droopy.

I played it classical music. Nothing.

I gave it sugar water. No change.

I ran an extension cord out the door to give it light, 24/7. No change.

Some days I demanded, others I pleaded: "Don't die on me! Come on Sunny, you can make it. Here, drink some spring water. You'll feel better!"

But beyond a certain point, all we can really do for another living being is give it our love and attention. We can only hope that with luck or fate or whatever else is on our side, whatever we give them is enough to help them through life.

And sometimes, if things really go our way, when they ask us for help, when they're open to our intercessions, we can do for them what they need. Even if they are sunflowers.

Nell gave me that chance one morning soon thereafter by letting me kiss her forehead and hold her in my arms. What's more, real words, spoken in the English language, were exchanged between the now sixteen-year-old and me.

She wasn't feeling well.

"Oh honey, are you okay?" I asked while making my move to pet her head and begin braiding her long brown wavy hair. She had her grandmother Donna's curls.

"No. I'm not ok. Please just hold me and don't let go."

And so I did. I held her in my arms for as long as she would let me.

"Do you want a cup of tea?" I asked about fifteen silent minutes of holding her and kissing her forehead later.

"Yes, please," she said, wrapped in a blanket and cuddling Clyde.

I figured this was as good time as any to show her the sunflower.

I brought her outside. "It's right over there," I said, pointing to the garden area by the front porch.

As Nell knelt by its stalk, she just looked at it and smiled.

"Daddy Flower," she said. "Let's name it Daddy Flower."

We both stood, marveling at everything the sunflower represented.

And while this was a perfect moment to check in with her about her father, to see how she was feeling, I didn't want to force that conversation.

Yet as each day passed, Daddy Flower got worse and worse. His leaves were turning more and more yellow; his stalk saggy and bending. Eventually, he became so weak that he could no longer hold up his own head. I made him a bandage out of sticks, gauze, and tape, but that wasn't helping, either.

Kate made another house call, and this time she wasn't quite so optimistic. "It has no more seeds," she pronounced.

"Is that a bad sign? Does it mean he's...I mean it's dead?"

"It's not good."

I could feel tears steaming in my eyes.

"There's not a lot you can do at this point, but just water it and see what happens."

Daddy Flower hung in there, until one day in early August, I found him flat on the ground. He had collapsed under his own weight.

The sunflower had dropped dead.

Shock. Disbelief. A freezing of emotion. Clear your head. Lean against a tree. Feel the hard cement on the ground, the cold night air on your face. Search the sky for that gray tunnel with the twinkly lights. Walk past the house. Go around the block. Just keep breathing.

Keep walking. Compose yourself. Fall against the house crying. Go buy a loosie from Deli Man.

Where is he? Where did he go? He was always here...

"You know the guy, Deli Man!" I said to the young man now standing behind the counter. "The guy who's worked here for like four years." I couldn't understand; it had only been five weeks since I had last seen him. "He's about this tall, with reading glasses that he props up on his head, but he doesn't read the newspaper because he doesn't trust the news—only books. Short brown hair. A little gray in the front. Brown eyes. He's kinda quiet until you get to know him. Then he talks a lot about philosophy. He has a degree in accounting and a thing for Isaac Newton, I guess because of the whole physics and math thing. Oh yeah, I forgot—he always has a pen protector in his pocket. If they ever leaked, his magic cleaning solution was hair spray. Him. That guy. I don't know his name..."

My voice trailed off. He clearly didn't know who or what I was talking about.

I went out of my way over the next few weeks to stop by or peer through the storefront glass to see if he was there, but he never came back.

Poof! Deli Man had gone up in a proverbial puff of smoke.

I felt that he had somehow been purposefully placed in my life, if only for the short time when I needed something the most.

Crazy, but...

59

Around the Internet in 80 Days

"Now excessive consciousness seems to be the problem. In a hall of mirrors, my mind reflects a multitude of images without distortion. Yet never grasping the object lesson of any one reflection, I find the clarity to be debilitating."

—Excerpted from Mark's journals

With summer now over, it was back to school and work. I also decided to go back on Match.com.

It didn't take long to learn that most online daters are just looking to try each other on, like shoes at a DSW outlet, not to buy and wear home. "So many to choose from!" they say. "Look at all the colors, shapes and sizes!"

The internet conditions us to want more and more choices, as if "more" or "newer" is the same thing as "better." Instant gratification—don't wait, buy today! If one thing doesn't work out right away, it's onto the next in an instant.

Compare, compare, compare. Despair, despair, despair.

We know deep inside that everything online is a filtered fabrication of reality, but we still fall for it. *Am I good enough?* we ask ourselves. How do I measure up? Wink at me! Favorite me! Like me! I don't even know you, but I need you to validate me! Me! Me! Me! Pick me!

The problem is, we're not sure what it is we are truly after. We easily overlook people in our search for the elusive "something more." That's why the odds of becoming one half of a matching pair are about the same on dating websites as they are in the animal kingdom, where only three percent of the roughly 5,000 mammalian species are known to be monogamous. Otters, prairie voles, beavers, foxes, wolves...and hairy tree-swinging gibbons. Otherwise, the vast majority of mammals are serial daters, too.

Yet knowing *all* of this, I still went for it. What's more, I let myself fall for a big game hunter, and ended up as Darius's kill.

At first, I wasn't really interested. I had already been on several dates—all of them nice but NFL (Not For Laura.) Okay, maybe I *was* sort-of interested in this Darius guy, but not really. But then, the first time we spoke on the phone, two hours had passed and we were still talking and laughing. That was a good sign.

But even so, it comes down to actually meeting, in person. That's when your hopes typically die, in that minute you see him sitting at a table for two and you're supposed to be the one.

I didn't plan on falling for him; in fact, I fought my feelings, as my attraction to him grew more and more intense over the next several months, until I became completely wrapped in his blanket of charisma.

"It's time," Darius said, looking at me with fiery intensity one night. The girls were at sleepovers...and I knew exactly what he meant.

It wasn't just the incredibly powerful chemistry where he took me like a dark stranger, filling me with a passion so deep, it felt like I'd never come down. It was that I had feelings for someone again.

Still, something inside kept telling me things were not quite right in Darius Land. I didn't want to listen, but I began to physically feel it—the tear between my heart and my head.

This is ridiculous, I thought. You've been dating for months. How could I sit there at a lovely romantic dinner or a weekend away together and go from being happy and fine to feeling anxious and vulnerable and then totally dejected in the days that followed?

Amy said it's all nature's fault. Women have higher levels of the feel-good hormone oxytocin in their reserves—as much as ten times more than men do. This is why we women tend to feel more bonded to our partners.

"Furthermore," she told me, "these elevated oxytocin levels can last for two days or more, giving the woman a greater sense of fusion with her partner, but also making her feel vulnerable." Amy called it a biological imperative, one where the woman has a physical need to feel cherished by the man she is with. This is why the rituals of romance, courtship, and the security of commitment feel so vital to a woman.

The problem, of course, is that men are the biological opposite to women in this way. Their oxytocin levels drop off shortly afterwards, at which point they're ready to leave the cave and get back to hunting the wooly mammoth.

So, that was it. I wasn't paranoid—I was suffering from love hangovers with Darius. Why didn't they teach this stuff in sex ed, or at least in high school biology?

At least my high school English teacher, Mrs. Lucky, hadn't failed me. She taught us that the most effective tragedies are punctuated by moments of comic relief, giving people a chance to recuperate emotionally before the next painful blow hit.

That's exactly what happened when I logged onto Match.com.

Not only did Darius still have his dating profile up, he was also "online now," according to the notification beaming at me from the computer screen.

Maybe the computer had made a mistake? Maybe he was "online now" because he was telling someone, "Thanks anyway." Or maybe he was checking to see if *I* was on?

I rationalized the facts, telling myself I should just enjoy dating. *Relax,* I would tell myself. Love takes time.

But then I began checking it regularly. Did he log on before or after we were together? Was it after we left for work together in the morning? During work? After dinner? What about Sundays? Tuesdays at 11:00? Fridays at 7:00? What were the patterns? *Were* there patterns?

One Saturday morning, he called at 9:00 am to "check in," saying he was driving down FDR Drive which was nowhere near his apartment, and another time when he said he had gone to the opera, my heart was no longer full of red juicy love. Instead, it was bleeding all over itself.

"It's either me or Match.com," I heard myself say.

Ask anyone and they will tell you to never give someone an ultimatum. It makes them run scared through the woods. I say, forget that. If there wasn't a problem in the first place, then you wouldn't have needed to *have* that talk in the second place, and you wouldn't have to break up with him in the third place, and then everyone wouldn't blame you for your own sadness in the fourth place. Either you are right for each other or you are wrong for each other, regardless of the reason. It's that simple.

It was Christmas Day.

Still, I got my miracle.

I knew Susannah would love the inflatable unicorn head I got her. I ducked into the RV to hide it before coming inside the house.

I found her sitting in the kitchen, red-eyed from crying.

"What's wrong?" I asked. No answer. "Are you alright?" I prodded.

"I'm just really sad, Mom," came the little reply.

"Why, honey?" I asked, stupidly. "Did something happen?"

The girls barely ever talked about Mark anymore. They would sooner let me see them naked in the shower than witness their deepest, most intimate emotions. That's why I didn't expect what Susannah said next.

"I miss Dad. A lot."

The only time they let me touch them anymore is if they're bleeding, throwing up, have fevers of more than 101°F, or if they are really, really, *really* upset.

Susannah let me hug her and hold her close.

I asked her if there was anything I could do to make it better. She looked up at me, all prickly faced, then launched into her imitation of a bratty, spoiled kid. "Get me a unicorn, Mommy. It's the only thing that will make me happy." Translation: "Nothing in this world exists that could possibly make me feel better." Or so she thought.

"Do you believe in magic, Susannah?" I asked.

She gave me an exhausted, quizzical look.

"Wait there. And do not move. I'll be right back," I instructed.

No time for shoes; I went barefoot through the snow to unearth the unicorn from its hiding spot.

"Close your eyes," I instructed, now back in the house. "Okay, now open them."

60

Just What the DR Ordered

"They were playing in the water, some diving
off cliffs. I put on some cut-offs and joined
in. Wily just goes to the nearest jumping-
off point and drops about 50 feet. He comes
out blue and sputtering. I guess I should
have told him the water came right out of the
mountains just above freezing."

—Excerpted from Mark's journals

Thanks to those wonderful things called American Express points, the girls and I were off to the Dominican Republic to visit my high school friend, Tricia, for the holiday.

Only now, I was doubly miserable as I sat on the airplane, freshly crushed over Darius while mentally preparing for a major sprinkling mission with Mark. (We had been there a few months after getting married; and it's where we learned I was pregnant with Nell.)

BE, I tried to tell myself. BE, BE, BE. Darius was nothing in the grand trajectory of my life. It was a minor setback that seemed major only because it had resurrected all of my grief. Darius had come to represent Mark, because I *needed* someone to represent Mark to me. And now, it was like losing Mark all over again.

In philosophy, Plato presents a mythology of love in which the original humans were freakishly self-satisfied creatures with four arms, four legs, two faces, etc. But they were considered a bit too smug, so the gods got to work splitting them each right down the middle, cursing us all to wander the earth miserably in search of our missing halves.

It makes for a good study in Philosophy 101. I can even see how such a tragically romantic metaphor would appeal to those with a poetic sensibility—especially the ones who have never been in love before.

But it didn't offer much comfort. Had losing Mark condemned me to live out the rest of my life as half a person? If I take a number, will they eventually assign me another other half? Is there only one person for each of us, and after that, are the rest of our relationships just a series of compromises?

And now here we were in the town of Cabarete, the four of us together—the girls, me and Mark-in-a Box. Susannah had found the adventure tour company herself, not knowing it was the same one her father and I used years ago.

Back then, I would have chosen lethal injection over jumping off thirty-foot cliffs into freezing cold pools of water. But now, somehow, here I was, a passenger in a van that was barreling up muddy hillsides into the Septentrional Mountain range, heading to a place called Ciguapa Falls.

Susannah set the rules for the jumps: no peeing in your pants, no puking, no freaking out, no trembling, and *no* calling for a helicopter.

"Man up mom!" Susannah shouted as I again clung to the side of a cliff.

Nell knew better than to join us; she had stayed poolside.

"Mom, if you don't jump now, you never will. *And* you're holding up the entire group." I looked back. A group of millennials were standing there not even puckering up for selfies. They were all waiting... for me... to go. Otherwise, I would ruin their shots.

Let me tell you: thirty feet doesn't seem so high until you're looking over the edge of it, especially when you're supposed to jump off it into a tiny pool of freezing cold water. And *especially,* especially when you have to do it ten more times to get to the end of the hike.

"Mom you have to jump. Okay? I'll count to three and then you jump. One, two, three..."

"No way! Do it in Spanish!" I told her.

She rolled her eyes. "Uno, dos, tres!"

There was no other choice. I had to jump. "Goodbye, cruel world," I called out before taking a running leap, Mark in hand. Mastering fear is empowering. Sure...Right...Never again...

A few days after jumping off waterfalls, it was jumping onto bikes for an intense yet exhilarating trek through the heart of the mountain range. It was the same ride Mark and I had done, including a swim in the Jamao River at the end. Then it was off to a really cool restaurant called the Blue Moon Inn for an exquisite poolside East Indian lunch. Mark loved this restaurant; it's an elegant tent where you sit on the floor to eat.

Sprinkle...

Another thing Mark never got to do in life was go zip lining. It wasn't a thing when he was alive, but he would have loved it. So when we found a 4,400-foot zip lining park, we were on it!

In Sosua Bay, his bones sunk right down into the snorkeling reefs, then Mark, the girls, and I traveled to a river called the Rio Yaque del Norte near Jarabacoa for a day of class III rapids "fun," capped off by a Dominican buffet, a.k.a. more chicken, at a ranch overlooking the river.

Our flight home got delayed for almost a week by the Arctic Vortex, a huge cold snap that froze the entire Northeast. There was no rush to get back anyway; Chuck was term-limited and out of office, meaning I was unemployed; my tenants were moving out; and there was no Darius to come home to.

Maybe that's why people say everything bad happens in threes; here I was, living proof that my life totally sucked unicorn ass.

61

Dancing in the Dark

"The words she spoke, the way she moved, the
life we shared stayed with me long after I
was gone. Our souls connected throughout
eternity even as she lived in her other
world and me in mine. The departure danced a
heavenly melody of solo midnights."

—Excerpted from Mark's journals

Sometimes, after everyone was asleep, I would go downstairs, take Mark off the bookshelf, and have long talks with him. Out loud. Is that insane? Sometimes I would just catch him up on everything that was happening with the girls, or I would read him the headlines, or a passage of a book I knew he would like. Other times, we'd slowly dance together in the living room. We still slept together sometimes when my king-sized bed felt impossibly large or when I had a cold.

"Who are you talking to?" Nell asked once when I thought we were alone. She and Susannah were peering over the stairway.

"Daddy." What else could I say?

"That's really weird, Mom. I hope you don't think he can hear you."

"Obviously I don't think he can hear me!"

"Then why are you talking to him?" Susannah asked.

"I don't really know. I know it's stupid, but I guess it's like visiting a grave. People talk to headstones when they visit graves, you know."

"I think it's sweet and I bet he can hear her," Susannah decided as they went back to bed.

A few nights later, I heard Nell in the living room. It was 11:30 at night, way past a reasonable bedtime.

"And then we went skiing, and you should have seen Susannah's wipeout," I heard her saying. "She's still not the best skier. But Mom got her back up and then we had hot chocolate in the lodge."

I was about to tell her to hang up the cell phone, get off the Internet or stop whatever electronic communication she was glued to when I realized who she was talking to. And as much as I wanted to listen in, it would have been like reading her diary. I closed my door and hoped Mark really could hear or somehow see how much those little girls missed him.

The longing for Mark made me miss Darius which made me miss Mark even more.

"I think I really almost loved him," I sniveled to Lisa over the phone. I was clearly having a relapse.

"You love the *idea* of Darius," she corrected. "You do not *love* him. You miss Mark and you tried to turn Darius into him to feel that love again. You know that, right?"

I actually did but just needed to hear it.

Unfortunately, there was nothing I could do about my new car.

62

Love Is *Not* What Makes a Subaru a Subaru

"The Flagstaff Cycle Center was where the guy in the pickup truck was good enough to drop us off. He said something about people who ride Hondas get 80 mpg. And how mine got 48. Harley hater."

—Excerpted from Mark's journals

Usually, it's the guy who buys a new car to impress women. I stupidly bought mine to impress what's his name.

In an act of widowhood bravery, I listened when he suggested trading in my big, green "Out of Africa"-style hemi engine four-wheel drive Jeep Commander for something smaller. The gas alone was costing me $350 a month, I reasoned. Plus, it was a constant reminder.

I settled on a black Subaru Forester, which was a fine car, but now every time I drove it, I felt guilty which made me miss Mark. I missed Darius, too. And the Jeep. And my life.

In short, I hated everything the car represented.

"Hi, Joe?" I called the salesman. "Is it too late to get the Commander back?"

"Too late, my love. It left the lot yesterday," he told me. I wondered if that was part of the advertising shtick, to call customers "love" to go along with the advertising campaign.

Great. Now I was mad at myself for making it a proving ground for a man who had no intention of going the extra mile with me.

Crash!

I'd backed right into a cement pole. Now I had a stupid car with a giant dent in it to remind me of my failures.

As it happened, Lucky Laura had a good day. It came in the form of a loud bang from the street, followed by a knock on the door. I stupidly hoped it was Darius, riding a white unicorn with a big bouquet of sunflowers in hand. What I got instead was a stoned teenage kid.

"Uh, I smashed into your car," he said as he stood there stammering, peering at me through red-rimmed eyes. "I'm really sorry. I didn't see your car parked there."

As we surveyed the somewhat substantial damage, his father drove up in a tow truck. It turned out that he owned an auto body repair shop in a nearby town and offered to fix the entire car, even the damage from my misadventure with the pole, in exchange for my not calling the police or insurance company.

Presto! Just like that, I had saved the $1,000 deductible, essentially through the art of procrastination.

If only my heart could be replaced as easily as a new bumper. But I did discover a few things about myself: specifically, what I don't want, what I don't need, and what I aim for. No doubt it *would* be hard to sleep alone, to battle one's own thoughts, to laugh, to stay motivated, to trust and love again.

But play is one thing, love is another. You can't play with love.

There are ways to deal with break-ups. Eat Twinkies. Volunteer at a local petting zoo. Call your mother. Take hot baths. Hang upside down to realign your back.

But in my case, I knew exactly what needed to be done, once and for all.

Part VI:
The Third
Trip: Kansas
Or Bust

63

Homeward Bound

"The stand went up, 750 ccs of motorcycle
roared to life and me with it. Time to get
out there and kick some major ass. Just me
and the highway."

—Excerpted from Mark's journals

The thing Mark needed most—which is also to say, what I needed
most—was to hit the Southwest and to return him to his boyhood
home in Kansas.

Even though it would be above 120 degrees and I would be
covering about 6,000 miles of dry desert heat, I had to do it.

Equally worrisome would be the 150-mile stretches of asphalt-
buckling roads with nothing but dust bowls, dead bugs, and dried
cacti to break up the landscape. No consistent cell phone service.
No consistent satellite reception for the GPS. No consistent water,
food, or gas. What if HaRVey broke down and we sat there boiling
to death for hours while waiting to flag down a passing car? What if
the people who stopped to help us instead attacked us? Cut the girls
heads off? Kidnapped us and locked us in a bomb shelter somewhere
in the desert?

You know, like my mom suggested could happen. Then what?

"I'll kick their asses," I joked with her on the phone.

"You sound just like Mark."

I'll take that as a compliment. But seriously, thanks for adding to my worry. It's not like I'm the only woman ever to take a road trip alone with her kids. Actually, three teenage kids; Nell was bringing a friend. And I brought Mark.

The time was now or never. Just do it. Go solo, girl. If you are going to truly move on with your life, you need to do this last trip. Let him go once and for all. BE free. BE normal (as if that was even possible.) BE done with grief.

64

On the Road Again

"I lit up a smoke and greased the chain,
checked the oil and tires. Got fuses. A flush
of friendship forms between them."

—Excerpted from Mark's journals

We hopped into HaRVey, waved goodbye to no one in particular, and headed for the Appalachian Mountains at Shenandoah National Park in West Virginia. This, of course, called for serenading Mark with "Take Me Home, Country Road" while hanging out the windows like the true redneck hooligans we had become.

And yes, there were ample sprinkles on Skyline Drive.

Then it was down to Atlanta, where we visited Stone Mountain, the largest high-relief sculpture in the world, and then for a stopover at my brother, Ted's house.

I knew our trusty steed HaRVey wasn't feeling well, as he chugged along puffing blue smoke out the exhaust pipe. But I had ignored his symptoms in hopes the clanking noise would go away, or that he at least wouldn't die until we got there.

"You can't go anywhere until you get this stuff fixed," Ted announced. He liked working on car engines, and HaRVey appeared to be his latest target. He started by buying all new tires at—where else—Costco, and then changing them out (even though they were brand new). He then spent four whole days wrestling with a sporadically broken generator. The clanking noise was also addressed in a separate repair involving a loose something-or-other.

We sat on the driveway talking for a few hours after that; about our childhoods and love and marriage and kids and life and everything. It was the first time we'd had a real conversation in years, without the backdrop of a big family gathering. I knew one thing for sure—I really loved my brother. He had my back.

And, rather than fill me with doom, gloom, and caution like everyone else had, he empowered me.

"I'm proud of you," he told me.

"Really?"

"Yes, really," Ted said. "What you are doing is such a testament to him. It's a little lopsided, but so are you. That's why everyone loves you."

HaRVey was now in top shape after several trips to the local Auto Zone store. Then came Ted's "RV 101" lessons.

"Do you know where the propane tank is?" he asked.

"I think so," I replied.

"This is how you turn it on and off."

"Okay."

"Tire pressure? You need to use this gauge to check the tires when they are cold, meaning not driven, every single morning. If they go below forty-five pounds, you have to fill them up."

"Okay."

"Show me you know how you start the generator from inside and outside the vehicle in case the switch doesn't work again."

"Okay."

"Water heater switch?"

"Check."

"Engine oil and antifreeze?"

"Check. It's that yellow dippy thing there. You said not to unscrew the cap when the engine is hot, right?" I said, feeling proud of myself for passing his test thus far.

"Tire iron? Lug nuts? Jack?"

"Check."

Next, he sat me down to plan out something of an itinerary, in case the GPS didn't work, and I found myself in all those predicaments my family and friends worried about—alone, out of gas, frying like an egg, and petrified in some forest.

With that, he gave us a few bags of groceries and wished us luck.

"You can do this, Laura," is the last thing he said to me.

The first stop on the third major sprinkling tour was in Nashville, where Mark now croons at the Country Music Hall of Fame; or where he now resides at the Grand Ole Opry in seat 21, row B. He would have died (ha-ha) to wear the $850 Tony Lama black caiman belly boots I sprinkled him in at a fancy bootery when no store clerks were looking. I wonder if whoever bought them ever wondered why there were ashes on his socks?

Then it was off to the National Civil Rights Museum in Memphis. Mark is there now; he was always a great believer in human equality. He's also now sitting on the bus with Rosa Parks and resting at the feet of MLK.

We went to Graceland, despite not being major Elvis fans. Shh... he's also in a book jacket at the presidential library.

And where else would a good wife sprinkle her husband but in the parking lot of the PJ's Men's Club for a little nudie action?

From there, we headed south to visit the Texas School Book Depository, where the girls learned about JFK's motorcade route through Dallas and the eventual assassination. Talk about conspiracy theories; what a perfect place for Mark.

Next, it was off to the Rodeo Cowboy Hall of Fame's Fort Worth Stockyards. We were not only sold on the idea of seeing a real rodeo, with cowboys and everything, but also learning that The Livestock Exchange Building was known as "The Wall Street of the West."

It seemed a most appropriate place for sprinkles, sprinkles, and more sprinkles.

65

Satan's Inferno

"And now it was hot. Simply walking made
you breathe hard. The heat distorted the
distance. Riding off the pavement. So hot the
stand stuck in the asphalt when you tried to
leave. Every time I stopped, I hosed myself,
clothes and all, and was dry again before
next gas stop."

— Excerpted from Mark's journals

I'd heard all the warnings about Texas heat, but never realized just how "hot" hot could be until the stupid generator—the thing that produced the air conditioning in the back of the RV—broke down. Again. That meant the girls and I were miserable, sweating to death and dehydrated for miles.

With the water and gas tanks nearing empty, just how far would it be until the next service station? Sixty miles? A hundred miles? One mile? Without GPS service, it was hard to tell.

We drove for endless miles through the singed brown desert terrain, no signs of life. Or gas. I'd suddenly never felt so lonely or alone in all my life.

It didn't help that the girls had "blocked" me from their lives by pulling the curtain closed between the driver's seat and the rest of the RV. That way, they could "talk" and have "privacy" while I drove in silence.

The decline started a few states back. They had begun rolling their eyes so far back in their heads whenever I spoke that I worried they'd get stuck there in the bowels of their little brains forever.

But what all this really meant was they were growing up and soon, they wouldn't need me or even want me around.

The realization left me despondent.

Temperatures continued to climb, hitting 121 degrees one early day when I stupidly didn't stop for gas after seeing a sign saying there was no gas for 115 miles. We had more than enough to get through the Guadalupe Mountains National Park. Or so I thought.

About an hour later, I realized the gas gauge had not moved. Great, that stopped working now too, as did the odometer. A rush of panic quickly followed.

Easy, Laura. Conscious breathing, remember? Is your breathing relaxed, rhythmic, silent, and deep? Now extend the exhale...that's it. It will be okay. You will get through it. Just breathe.

I didn't need Ted to tell me what the engine's hesitation meant—we were definitely about to run out, right there on a death-dry road in the Chihuahuan desert. It was 11 am on a Sunday morning, no cars in sight; only an odd brittlebush to break up the emptiness as the sun blasted through HaRVey's aluminum siding. We were alone in a bone-dry basin. Sweating.

There was no need for emergency flashers. Nothing in sight, not a bird, not a speck of life. An hour passed. Still nothing.

It was so hot the tires almost melted into the road. A decision had to be made. Do we empty our water tank and coast down the hills to save precious gas or do we save the water just in case we break down?

Thankfully, the big white truck I thought I saw coming toward us was real, as was the woman driving it. She said there was a café about five miles ahead and that it probably had gas. She would follow us, just in case.

The café owner, a short, sun-cracked man who'd clearly seen too many fields go fallow in the hot summer heat, kindly offered me two gallons for $30, but only if he had extra in the storage shed.

"Happens here all the time," he mumbled, shuffling his way to the shed. "I shoulda opened a gas station instead."

Or a loan shark office, I wanted to say.

The woman pulled me aside. "That's highway robbery!" she exclaimed, offering to follow me into town.

Lucky Laura strikes again. As did Mark—right on the bumper of her truck after hugging and thanking her at the gas station.

Something inexplicable then drew us to Hobbs, New Mexico. A profound feeling of déjà vu came over me and stayed—a feeling so strong it either *meant* something...or I was suffering from temporal lobe epilepsy. Suddenly, I remembered it was the birthplace of Mark's step-mother.

The same thing happened in the giant limestone caves at Carlsbad Caverns, and the feeling followed us to the White Sands National Monument. But it was quickly overtaken by the wonder of it all. There was no place else like this on Earth; in fact, it felt more like Mars. Giant wave-like dunes of gypsum sand engulfed the earth making everything stark white and windswept except for the shadowy outlines of our bodies rolling down the hills like human cigars.

66

What Is Good

"Sedona's a couple of hours away, in the heart
of Oak Creek Canyon, down a mountainside
lined with burning pines. They had a forest
fire. Lost thousands of acres. Back down the
canyon floor, we pull into an area called
Grasshopper Point, a hangout for the locals.
We swim under the waterfall, the sound of
this hippy guy drumming bouncing off the
mountains."

—Excerpted from Mark's journals

We had many teachers along the way. One was a grandmother we
met running a roadside taco stand on our way to Jemez Falls,
New Mexico. The trust she placed in me to let her three young granddaughters come exploring with us proved there was good left in the
world. We packed in the RV together and became a party of six—ages
eleven, twelve, thirteen, fourteen, fifteen, sixteen, and fifty—and spent
the day exploring their secret spots in the red rock cliffs, soaking in
the natural hot springs, and swimming under a rushing waterfall.

We got back to the pueblo after sundown and sat with the entire
family, all twenty-three of them, singing and dancing and eating rice

and beans and sugary fried cakes with cherries until it was near mid-night. The grandmother handed me a loaf of bread that she had made in the outdoor horno oven. It was her gift to us, and as she hugged me goodbye, she whispered: "Hold onto what is good, even if it is a handful of earth."

We then headed west into Arizona, and then down the insanely steep mountain roads into Oak Creek Canyon. It wasn't easy getting there, on account of more wildfires, but this time, there was no one to stop me.

Mark *must have* gone to Sedona on his motorcycle trip; now we could hit at least one place he had stepped foot on or burned rubber. All we needed was for HaRVey to hold out on the insanely steep mountain passes where the last remnants of heavy winds and dense, dry timber had just fueled a blaze that spread across 4,500 acres in the span of twenty-four hours. The fire had been out for more than a week, lucky for everyone.

We made it! Yeah HaRVey! We needed a vacation from our vacation and immediately signed up for one of those dreadful timeshare condos where you stay for free, complete with hot dogs, a swimming pool and real beds, in exchange for a pressure-filled "sales" presentation. (I also snuck in a free frozen margarita at the hotel bar, Bad Girl Scout Leader!)

Though it was close to the worst two hours of my life, getting yelled at by the salesperson for saying no, I would not be buying a timeshare today, tomorrow or next year, it was worth it for the free night of accommodation.

Escaping through a side door, we waved down a couple in a white Jeep to whisk us off to the parking lot where HaRVey sat waiting. We asked for directions to a swimming hole I read about in a tourism guide. No, no, no they said. Follow us! Grasshopper Point was a swimming hole known only to locals where we spent the day swimming and lazing by the water's edge.

Stephen told us he was a shaman. *(Of course, he was a shaman. Wasn't everyone in Sedona a shaman?)* At first, when he started doing his "spiritual drumming" thing, it seemed so contrived. But as I laid back in the water, letting the rhythm of drums reverberate in the ripples of water, I floated into the deepest peace I had ever felt in my life. Calm...peaceful...trance-like sleepy floating.

And sure, why wouldn't we get up at 5 am the next day to hike to a cave in the Red Rock mountains, okay girls? Stephen's friend Greta met us on the roadside wearing full-on spiritual bling—a lasso of crystals, beads, rawhide, and silver, complete with a bandanna—the essence of a spiritual Ivory Girl. Stephen came walking through the desert seemingly out of nowhere, carrying a shoulder bag made of wolf fur that he had filled with special accoutrements such as sage leaves, incense, and spirit water.

The girls and me? We brought peanut butter and jelly sandwiches.

Up the hiking trail we went, which led us to the Bell Tower, a majestic red rock mountain. The hike was just the right amount of "don't look down" where you couldn't help taking in the stunningly scenic desert vistas, especially from way up high.

We would be making a stop by his secret cave to do some spiritual cleansings...and sprinkles.

We welcomed all kinds of cleansing, spiritual or soapy, and are always up for a good adventure. So was a hawk that appeared as we neared the cave. Stephen was overjoyed, saying it was one of our ancestors. I just hoped it wouldn't bite us.

"Are you girls ready?" Stephen asked. His manner was gentle and kind, much like Deli Man's. The girls took an immediate liking to him.

"What's a shaman?" Nell whispered to me, a little out of breath, as we entered the dark dwelling.

Stephen explained that his job was to guide people to inner truths and power.

First, he would need to smudge us in order to clear our paths toward enlightenment. That's when you sit or stand with arms out, eyes closed, while letting the smoke of burning sage leaves wash over your body while the practitioner, in our case Stephen, interacts with spirits. He explained that the cleansing washes away any negative conditions, opening the way for positive experiences.

We were then "cleared" to enter the cave. Phew! He handed each of us our own drum and led us in chant. Amah... Wuhu...Mmm... Ommmmmm...

Now came the fun part. Getting our cards read. Nell chose the Swan card. You could tell this pleased Stephen. He said it meant she had great energy and a positive outlook to "bestow upon all she walked with in life."

He looked deeply into her eyes, telling her how the Swan signifies a profound spiritual devotion and exudes the essence of angels who impart divine healing words and energies on all they meet. "It is a reminder of the possibility of transformation of something or some-one," he said.

Susannah's card was the Ace of Wands, a torch that would guide her throughout her life. Stephen told her that she would need to carry that torch with her to light her way to happiness, but that the Ace could not tell her exactly *where* to go; it could only guide her to make good choices.

I pulled the Lovers card.

"You have the strength and confidence to overcome all obstacles in life through the bond that the two lovers have created. It's incredibly strong and is often reflective of a marriage, a soul mate connection, or a very intimate and close relationship," he told me. "This is a time when you are figuring out what you stand for and what your personal philosophy on life is."

At that moment, I thought he descended from the heavens. And I wanted to tell him everything. But I didn't, figuring if he were truly spiritually connected, an angel would have already told him we had been blinded by death and were on the road to acceptance or whatever.

I just smiled.

When it was time to say goodbye, Stephen pulled me aside while Greta led the girls down the mountain.

"I don't mean to upset you," he said, "but you will come to understand that you are on a personal journey, Laura, and that you are not alone in it. I can feel a man, perhaps a husband, or someone very important in your life, is here with us now. I didn't want to upset you in front of the girls...He's been with us the whole time. That's why Greta and I pulled over in the first place. He was calling to me. He wants you to know he is still with you. He will help guide you. He is protecting you. And he is in love with you and says he will never leave you, even though he is on the other side."

I would normally shun such spiritual revelations, but it was as if there were now cracks of light where sunflowers could grow.

"You are doing the most beautiful thing for him, you and the girls," he said as he and Greta hugged and kissed us goodbye, and then their faces slowly got smaller and smaller before disappearing in the rear-view mirror.

67

From FOC to FOM

"Who knows how many bones lay beneath the
tableland of the Hopi Mesa and butte, the
skeletons of a stormy past. A dog appeared as
I closed my eyes, its yellow tail wagging. A
friendship seems to envelop this lonely dry
spot and this dog would become a constant
companion. She reaches, throws a driftwood
shard for dog fetching. Dog's feet in the
foamy water, stick in mouth, races back to
master who pats him on the head and strokes
his chin. She tosses it back out again."

—Excerpted from Mark's journals

"Please, Mom, can we keep him?" Susannah pleaded.

"No," I said without looking up from my iPhone. I saw
the dog approach her but was still trying to figure out why I had
really just driven 300 non-stop miles in the opposite direction for...
absolutely nothing.

"Does this sound accurate to you?" I asked Nell, not really
expecting a response.

I read the website out loud anyway, just to make sure wc were in the right place:

"'Welcome. You have come to Hopi Land. We Hopi are known for having lived here as a people continuously from ancient time. Where we are located today in present day Arizona is where we have always lived, with roots back in time to some one hundred generations in our land. Our culture, therefore, is one of the first (oldest) on the continent.'" It went on to describe its cultural center, artisans, and traditional Wednesday night dances.

"Are you kidding me?" I snorted, blaming Google for luring us to an empty parking lot in the middle of the desert. "You call this sacred land? This is what you call the old bait and switch, girls. Do *you* see any Indians? No. There are no Indians. Do you see any native dancers? There *are* no native dancers. Do you see any artisans? There are *no* artisans."

The cultural center looked cool, but it was closed. There *was* a well-lit diner and small hotel, but a few stray dogs were hanging around. And you know what that means; I was *not* getting out.

"Mom, it's politically incorrect to call them Indians," Nell said, dismissing my rant. "They are called Native Americans."

"Yeah, well, only to outsiders," I retorted, rolling down the window to throw some ashes on the ground. It was an obligatory sprinkle, a we-drove-all-this-way-for-nothing sprinkle. "You think they call *themselves* Native Americans? No, they call themselves Indians, as in 'Yo, Indian, what up?'"

This cracked me up, which only annoyed Nell more.

"Mom, why do you think you are so funny?"

"Because I *am* so funny, Little Blue Sky Eagle Foot," I shot back, collapsing in laughter on the RV floor. Nell's friend Anna began laughing, but quickly buried her face in a pillow. She knew that siding with the mother had the potential for a *Lord of the Flies*-style outcome.

Susannah, meanwhile, was totally focusing on the newest object of her affection—a big yellow dog with a white spot on its chest.

She had already passed the "Can we keep it" phase and was moving toward the "But Mom" phase.

"But Mom," she protested, tugging at my shirt and giving me her best puppy dog eyes. "Look at him. He's obviously stray. He was just eating gross leftover chicken bones out of that dumpster."

"There are starving children all over the world, Susannah, worry about them instead," I told her. "In fact, why don't you send them all the raisins you picked out of your cereal yesterday? I'm sure they would be thrilled to have raisins in their bran."

The dog just stood there, looking directly at me. For some reason, I was not afraid of it and walked straight over to pet it.

The "But Mom" had failed. Time for "Bargaining."

"I promise to feed and walk him every day," she said. She sounded like she really believed her words.

"When was the last time you walked Clydezilla?" I fired back, as the dog rolled on its back. "Wait, I can answer that for you. How 'bout never?" I shook my head. "No more dogs, Susannah. You don't walk them, and I end up having to do it."

Clyde had been our Christmas-holiday-alone, I-feel-sorry-for-my-kids-but-this-cute-little-puppy-will-make-them-happier (mistake) present.

"Please stop calling him Clydezilla, Mom," she argued. "His name is Clyde. And I also *know* what FOC stands for," she added. "I hear you say it to him under your breath all the time."

I pretended not to hear her.

"It stands for f-off Clyde," she announced. "I'm fourteen, you know; I'm not stupid."

I prayed my beautiful, blond flower-field girl would not transform into a Daisy Dukes- wearing, bad grade-getting, I'm so bored

FaceSnapInstaChatGramming, selfie-taking rebellious droid—better known as a full-blown teenager.

Worse yet, she was a *girl* teenager.

"Susannah," I warned her, in my best stern mother/father tone. "Don't swear. It's not ladylike."

"But you swear at the dog all the time," she protested. "And you're a mother!"

"And I'd probably swear at this dog, too."

"FOM," I heard her whisper under her breath.

"Don't you say that to me, young lady!"

"I didn't, Mom. I would never say that to you. I just named the dog Mesa, after the Hopi Mesa Indian Reservation," she said eagerly as the dog lazily rolled over on her lap, all four giant paws in the air with a loping smile on his face. "I just wanted to hear how it would sound when you say it."

She was now going for the guilt jugular.

"Imagine if poor little Clyde got lost out here like this and had to live wild in the desert?" she continued. "Then what? Would you want a family to just leave him here like that?"

"I'd pay good money for that," I replied. "Did you know he ate my new Steve Madden outlet store boots before we left? I loved those boots, almost as much as I hate Clyde right now. The answer is a big, fat N-O. No more shoe-eating, floor-peeing dogs!"

Nell was always way ahead of everyone and was already gathering intelligence on the dog from the kitchen staff. Turns out, it had been hanging around the grounds for around three years. He definitely didn't have an owner. He was a nice dog; never bit anyone, played well with the other dogs. Everyone loved him!

"I'm sure he's lovely," I said upon receiving this detailed report, "but I am not driving across the rest of country with three teenagers, all their—ahem—clothes, and this giant dog in a two-by-six living space," I said.

As the dog continued to stare at me with pleading brown eyes, I knew I was only trying to convince myself. There was something about him; something deeply connective and meaningful. It felt as though he had a human's soul; leaving him would have been like leaving your grandfather on the side of the highway.

68

The Best Dog in
the World

"Sometimes connections are made that deepen
the groundings of life. Those are the
inexplicable truths of the swords that we
either live by or die by, the ones that stand
by our sides."

—Excerpted from Mark's journals

Mesa had hitchhiked his way into the family, and we had fallen more and more in doggie love with him with each wag of his giant tail.

The best was watching Susannah teach him to swim in Lake Powell. Beachgoers cheered after watching her pick up and drag all eighty-two pounds of him into the water before he finally learned to do the doggie paddle. He never tired of playing fetch with the driftwood on the beach; back and forth he ran until night fell.

Then we were onto Hoover Dam, and then Zion and Bryce Canyon where Mesa proudly walked by our sides without a leash, giving out presidential kisses to everyone who passed. At night, the girls would pile into a sleepy heap of paws, arms, and legs as they cuddled up with him in front of our camp fires. He was my constant front seat companion as we rolled down the highway. Sometimes I swear he knew what I was thinking… and feeling.

He was truly the best dog in the world.

It wasn't until I saw the expression on the veterinarian's face that I realized something was wrong, that the spots of blood on the RV floor were not from a small cut on his foot.

I knew that look: the "I am now going to turn off my emotions in order to tell this woman something really, really bad that is going to make her cry a lot" look.

"Cancer? You're kidding me, right?" I pleaded, as if that would change the diagnosis.

The vet said it was a TVT Canine Tumor, a common problem in third-world or stray dogs. The tumors are internal (located on the genitals), so you can't see them. But they were there, he said.

I guess Mesa was a little "wilder" than we had thought.

We'd end up taking him to three different vets for three different opinions. They all said the same thing. It would be best to put him to sleep; way cheaper and easier than chemotherapy, which wasn't totally proven to work on this type of cancer. None of them had ever treated a tumor like his, either.

A few tear-filled tissues later, my mind was made up.

We got Mesa the biggest bone we could find…and started the chemo treatments.

The Animal Medical Center thought it would take around three rounds to shrink the tumor if it was going to work at all. It ended up taking thirteen treatments to kill it off. And while I didn't have that kind of money laying around, I found ways to save it and raise it (thanks to an angel named Bee Tosh) and slowly pay off the rest on my credit card.

Everyone thought I was crazy to not just put him on a plane and return him to the reservation.

Kim's the one who turned to me one day and said, "You think this dog is Mark reincarnated, don't you? You think Mark came back as a dog! You do, right? That's why you're doing this!"

She had meant it as a joke, but when I thought about it, it was actually a little true. Not that I thought the dog was Mark, just that there was something about him that made me feel super connected to Mark. It was something about his eyes and the way he looked at us, like he had been waiting a long time for us to find him and bring him home.

One thing was for sure.

We would need a lot of "Hopi" for Mesa.

69

Hail to the Gonzo Faithfuls

"Late afternoon fading to nightfall, us
breezing down out of Denver, onto the flat
of eastern Colorado on I-70. Night wraps
before we hit the Kansas line. A warm breath,
pavement still hot from the day. Maybe it's
not so much the miles but the process. The
road as metaphor to the end that awaits us
all."

—Excerpted from Mark's journals

Like so many other Gonzo Faithfuls, we traveled to Aspen, Colorado, home of Owl Farm—the forty-two-acre property where Hunter Thompson lived, wrote, and raised peacocks from the mid-1960s until he died in 2005.

While not usually one for following rules, I was not about to pull a fast one on his widow by ignoring the smattering of No Trespassing and Keep Out signs posted to the fence. Instead, we politely and respectfully sprinkled Mark throughout the pages of *Fear and*

Loathing in Las Vegas and left it on the roadside by the entrance to the property before quietly pulling away.

The closest we got to Thompson was at the J-Bar in Aspen's oldest hotel, which happened to be one of his haunts. I read that he would go to the post office to pick up his mail and be there by noon to divide his correspondence into three piles—bills, fan mail, and periodicals. Then he would order his food and drinks for the whole day and line it up next to the stacks of sorted mail.

For the first pile, he'd have eggs, bacon, coffee, toast, and a Bloody Mary; for the second pile, he'd have a cheeseburger and fries, washed down with a bottle of beer; and for the third and final pile, he'd have pasta and a bottle of red wine.

We got the eggs and bacon.

The best place, however, to soak up some counterculture was in his former drinking den, the Woody Creek Tavern. A short drive from Aspen, it was next to a trailer park, very far removed from all the glitz and glamour. The walls were covered with photos and press clippings about local residents, but mainly Thompson. I sprinkled Mark under a barstool before sitting down to order his favorites: a burger and green chili pork.

Having paid homage to Thompson and now to Mark, we visited Denver for a few days and then we continued onto I-70 for nine straight hours, until we finally reached the Kansas state line.

70

There's No Place
Like Home

"Samuel looked up from his plowing, wiped his
brow with the back of his hand, while a mule
idly flicked flies with its tail. Hot Kansas
sunburned his bare back, hard chunks of soil
filled his boots. He saw the lone slight
figure making his way across the south end of
the furrowed field toward the cabin: Isaac.
His first-born son."

—Excerpted from Mark's journals

It seemed poetic justice to end the trip here, where Mark's life began. But first, we'd visit my cousin Scott's farm outside of Wichita for a few days. I had been to rural farms before, but this came close to winning the blue ribbon at the country fair. No street name, just go left at the gas station and follow the road until you see a big white beautiful farmhouse.

There were hugs and hellos all around. We hadn't seen each other since childhood, but the years instantly melted away as if no time had passed. Soon the house was filled with even more family, including my Aunt Sally, the reverend who led Mark's funeral, and her sister Mary, who drove three hours to see us. My aunt is like that. She stops at nothing for family.

After lunch, the girls fed and groomed as many animals as they could get their hands on, from horses to bunny rabbits, in between climbing the apple trees.

"We're in heaven," Nell told me, eyes filled with love as she snuggled a brand-new baby pig.

We stayed two nights and considered another, but something told me to go visit Mark's father and his wife, Latrell, although it would only be for a quick overnight. Otherwise, we wouldn't see them until June. Mark's mother and her husband always came in April. The only time that schedule had changed in fifteen years was when both sets of parents *somehow* ended up visiting within days of each other in November, just days before Mark died.

Mark's father took us to the house where Mark had grown up. Three ladies were standing in the front yard talking by the mailbox. The girls were too embarrassed to get out of the car, and I think Warren, Mark's father, felt awkward, too.

But I was not about to turn back now. I approached them alone (well, almost alone; I had Mark-in-a-Box in hand).

"Excuse me," I said. They probably figured I was selling Bibles, given the number of churches we had seen and that I was wearing a dress.

"My husband—I mean, my late husband—was raised in this house," I explained. "I was wondering if it's okay if I go back to the creek bed to sprinkle some of his ashes?"

The woman held her hand out to me, leading me to the back of the house and down the hill to sit in the grass. So this was it. This was where Mark spent his life.

As I watched the water trickle through the storm drain pipe that led to the creek, I closed my eyes trying to imagine Mark and his brothers throwing mud pies at each other, building their forts and digging for worms to go fishing with their dad and Uncle Jerry.

I could almost see him racing his red bike through the neighborhood, waving to the neighbors on his paper route or sitting in his bedroom looking out the window. Even though the curtains were now striped, I knew which room belonged to him.

As I sprinkled him in the creek and all around the house, I hoped Mark would experience the same feeling I had sitting under the apple tree at my own childhood home. Perhaps he had just one more frog to catch or one more slingshot to fire.

I wonder if his father sat watching or if he turned away. It's something I will never know and something I hope he never forgets—that love guides us even when we sometimes feel hopeless and lost.

71

Sunflower Fields Forever

"Wanting is suffering. The Four Noble Truths.
1) Life is suffering. 2) Suffering is due to
attachment. 3) Attachment can be overcome by
certain spiritual techniques and knowledge.
4) The eightfold path can accomplish this and
achieve nirvana."

—Excerpted from Mark's journals

A few weeks later, Mark's step-mother was told she was going to die. Cancer, age seventy-four.

"You are doing everything that she needs and wants from you," I told his father, trying to console him as he described taking care of her. "She will want to die in your arms, and it will be one of the most beautiful tributes to your relationship. You will see, although I know you can't possibly understand this now."

As for me, my beautiful tribute was almost complete. There was just one place left for Mark to go—in that giant field of Kansas sunflowers.

They weren't hard to find—they were everywhere. But there was one specific field I needed to find, the one he led me into blindfolded on that gorgeous I-love-you day.

Finding the exact field was easy. It's a place I will always see in my mind's eye, about 1.4 miles past the blue house on the corner.

This was the one time I needed to be strongest. For him. For me. For our families. But mostly for the girls.

The time had come to say goodbye. He was home now.

The girls and I fell silent as we dug into the box, bracing ourselves against the beauty of the waving yellow field. Loosening my hold, I let the bony grit slip through the spaces between my fingers as I started the countdown.

"One!"

"Two!" Nell called out.

"Three!" Susannah cheered.

We drew our arms across our hearts, and then let him fly up and out, over the sun-kissed field and into the bright blue sky.

Epilogue

Throughout all our struggles, life can only give you chances. You're the one who has to search for and find your own answers. Moreover, your conclusions or truths can change over time. The important thing is to think about whatever it is and then think about it some more. That's the beginning of understanding—whatever teaches us to talk to ourselves; whatever teaches us to drive our way out of despair; whatever allows us to speak to each other across time.

Ashes. Dusty, bony ashes. Black boxes and car headlights on the highway. Illusions beyond truth. It's where the mind strikes reality and you're faced with it all: the things that rip at your guts and make you want to lay down in a field to die. Alone. Step away for a moment and the illusion comes back, life-love-never-dying. Here and gone. There and not there. Love and not love. Photographs on the wall. The faces of the people who have passed through our lives. His gray coat still hanging in the closet.

These are the hard, lonely truths.

Life is short. And fate can be cruel. Sometimes we don't even want to be here, but we have to immerse ourselves in this life anyway. With hearts open. We get up and do it again. Go to work. Come home. Make dinner. Sleep.

That is the privilege of the living.

We love what death and despair doesn't touch. We pull each other from life's wreckage to avoid the pain of the loss and the sick and the sadness. To go forward.

I'm not sure why Mark chose me, but he did. He was my love, my teacher. These are the things that are immeasurable. The things that are so glaring when you slow down. When you stop running. When you stop chasing fear.

That is when you truly live a life.

How does a person know when they've finally healed from a wound so deep they thought it would never close? Letting go can't possibly mean that the love itself dries up and blows away. That's not healing; that's forgetting. If the love is there and is real, then it can't possibly be forgotten, even over time.

But maybe it *is* possible to let go, eventually, of the desperate fear of love's imaginary impermanence. Maybe we can learn to look only at the now of it all, and *perhaps* a little further forward, rather than forever backward, knowing that our love will always be right where we left it. In our hearts and on our pillows.

Is it really gone, or has it just changed form? Are the inexplicable coincidences meant to be recognized as possible signs of life ever after? Is it determination or destiny?

All of these big existential questions were answered through the accidental guide to my salvation. Mark's journal.

Some people believe we have lived and died many times, but don't remember our former lives because our soul's memories are not transferred to our baby brains at birth. They say that what we know in the current life is a partial memory of things we learned in past lifetimes. That we are cleared of all past prejudices, learning blocks, and wrong teachings, and are ready for a fresh start—just like a new term in school. And, like school, when we have learned enough of life's lessons, we graduate and don't have to come back to this earth anymore, except as volunteers to teach stragglers.

Throughout this life, I've learned we don't get to choose what we want or don't want to happen, and that the level of hurt and pain you suffer does not justify loss. I've seen how you can want something so badly that you can't even see that it's killing you not to have it, how you can do everything possible to stop something just for it to happen anyway.

In the end, there is no way of truly knowing what tempts our minds to believe. For me, for now, this is the way I choose to see death—as a sequence of life everlasting.